RISEN AND WITH YOU ALWAYS

242.36
L43r

NOTRE DAME MOTHERHOUSE
READING ROOM

RISEN AND WITH YOU ALWAYS
†

Emeric Lawrence
O.S.B.

Daily
Meditations
for the
Easter
Season
Masses

THE LITURGICAL PRESS
St. John's Abbey • Collegeville, MN 56321

Cover design by Janice St. Marie

Nihil obstat: Robert C. Harren, J.C.L., *Censor deputatus.*
Imprimatur: ✝George H. Speltz, D.D., Bishop of St. Cloud, February 5, 1986.
Excerpts from the English translation of *The Roman Missal* © 1973, 1985, International Committee on English in the Liturgy, Inc. All rights reserved.

Scripture texts used in this work are taken from the NEW AMERICAN BIBLE and LECTIONARY FOR MASS, copyright © 1970 by the Confraternity of Christian Doctrine, Washington, D.C., and are used by license of said copyright owner. No part of the NEW AMERICAN BIBLE may be reproduced in any form without permission in writing. All rights reserved.

Copyright © 1986 by The Order of St. Benedict, Inc., Collegeville, Minnesota. All rights reserved. No part of this book may be reproduced or transmitted in any form or by any means, electronic or mechanical, including photocopying, recording, taping, or any information storage and retrieval system, without the permission of The Liturgical Press.

Printed in the United States of America.

1	2	3	4	5	6	7	8	9

Library of Congress Cataloging-In-Publication Data

Lawrence, Emeric Anthony, 1908–
  Risen and with you always.
  1. Eastertide—Meditations. I. Title.
BV55.L39 1986   242'.36   86-2826
ISBN 0-8146-1448-5

RISEN AND WITH YOU ALWAYS

THE EASTER SEASON

This is the third book in a series of meditations on the daily Masses of the three seasons of the Church year—Advent, Lent, and now the Easter Season. For over half a year we have been following the life of Jesus Christ as it has been made present for us in the daily liturgy. Hopefully these books have given their readers a deeper insight into Jesus and his Word and work that a greater intimacy with him will have resulted. Above all I hope that a vivid sense of Christ's merciful presence has grown.

It will be well if the reader is not satisfied with an initial reading of the books but that the books will resemble the liturgical seasons themselves and always seem like a new beginning. I believe that this hope will be achieved if these daily meditations will provide "takeoffs" for further personal delving into the texts on the part of the reader. The texts, especially the readings, are inexhaustible, like the Jesus they point to or describe.

The title for this final book of the series was not hard to determine, mainly because of the Easter Sunday morning I experienced in Jerusalem in 1962. I was part of an ecumenical pilgrimage to the Holy Land led by two Protestant ministers and two French Dominican priests, the group numbering about three dozen Catholics and Protestants from the Low Countries, Germany, and France. That morning I celebrated Mass in one of the Roman Catholic churches in Jerusalem, and shortly after the Mass I stood with the group on the top of the Mount of Olives, looking down on the sun-bathed holy city, the words of the Introit of the Easter Mass still fresh in my mind and heart: "I have risen and am with you still." One of the ministers said with deep reverence: "This is an Easter you will never forget." And he was right, not only because of the view but most of all because of those words: "I have risen and am with you still." To that I can only add: Alleluia, alleluia, alleluia!

Emeric A. Lawrence, O.S.B.

43 EASTER SUNDAY

READING I Acts 10:34, 37-43   **READING II** Col 3:1-4
GOSPEL John 20:1-9

Reading I: Peter concludes his address on the first Pentecost to the crowds of Jerusalem. He relates Jesus' last days and his commission to the twelve.

Reading II: Paul tells the Colossians that in baptism they have died and risen with Christ, and he points to the final day when we shall appear with him in glory.

Gospel: Mary Magdalen discovers Jesus' empty tomb, runs to tell the Apostles Peter and John, who in turn run to the tomb and find Mary's claim verified.

I have risen: I am with you once more (Entrance Antiphon).

May we never forget: Jesus is with us once more, with us still, never more to leave us by ourselves, alone. Today we come to the climax, the goal of Lent, the goal of our Christian life, indeed, the goal of all history. As all the thousands of years of humankind's hope and desire for ultimate deliverance, peace, joy, and fullness of love come to a head in Christ and his triumphant resurrection, so do our hope and desire come to a head in Christ's triumph today.

Christ has become our paschal sacrifice;
let us feast with joy in the Lord (Gospel Verse).

The resurrection of Jesus is the ultimate fulfillment of the deepest desire of human hearts. We thirst for the *living* God, the fullness of joy, peace, love, truth. Jesus is the living God! His resurrection proves it: "I have risen: I am with you once more."

As the hind longs for the running waters,
so my soul longs for you, O God.
Athirst is my soul for God, the living God (Ps 42:2-3).

"You are looking for Jesus of Nazareth, the one who was crucified. He has been raised up; he is not here" (Mark 16:6).

Jesus is no longer in the tomb; he has been raised and is now the heart or life principle of his Body, the Church. Those of you who attended the Easter Vigil service will recall how the Easter candle, the symbol of the risen Christ, entered the darkened church, and soon the one light from that candle spread to the candles in the hands of all who were present. There was one heart beating, the heart of the risen Savior. In him we were all one living body, one family. It is so much better to have him with and in us than to have him in the tomb;

for now we know the end and goal of all our seeking and hoping. We know it in the joy of possession.

So Lent is over for another year, and no one can blame us if we are all a bit relieved. But it might well be worthwhile for us to question ourselves about the difference—or lack of difference—Lent has achieved in our lives. Have we made any progress in our effort to die to selfishness, lack of charity and understanding, or indifference to the feelings and needs of others? Above all, has our desire for God intensified during this period? We may well recall the Opening Prayer we heard on Tuesday of the First Week of Lent:

> Father,
> look on us, your children.
> Through the discipline of Lent
> help us to grow in our desire for you.

Growth in desire for our God is the ultimate proof of a blessed Lent.

Even though this Mass is full of joy, praise, and exultation, Mother Church does not forget that we, her children, remain face-to-face with daily living in our world, our families, our particular vocations, our struggles and agonies, as well as our joys. Easter is springtime, and springtime brings new life. It is the time of hope, a time that always points to the future, to a harvest, to a re-created, renewed world. And for each of us, the daily dying to self we tried to experience during Lent points to our personal final dying with Christ at the end of our life in this world. So being a thoughtful, farseeing mother, the Church prays with and for us today:

> God our Father,
> by raising Christ your Son
> you conquered the power of death
> and opened for us the way to eternal life.
> Let our celebration today
> raise us up and renew our lives
> by the Spirit that is within us (Opening Prayer).

But the Prayer after Communion can be the best and most needful of all:

> Father of love,
> watch over your Church and bring us to the glory of the resurrection promised by this Easter sacrament.

May we all come with joy to that feast which lasts forever. Amen!

261 MONDAY OF THE OCTAVE OF EASTER

READING I   Acts 2:14, 22-32
GOSPEL   Matt 28:8-15

Reading I: After receiving the Holy Spirit on Pentecost, Peter reviews the life of Jesus for his hearers, including the prophecies of his coming, his life, work, death, and his resurrection.

Gospel: Matthew tells how Jesus appears to the women who had come to the tomb, tells them not to be afraid but to carry the good news to the apostles.

There may well be special significance for our time in the fact that Jesus first appeared to women, not to the chosen apostles. And there is extra significance in his commission to them to carry the news of his resurrection to the men locked up in that upper room for fear of their lives. The women become apostles to the apostles—no insignificant honor, that! One reason, I am sure, is simply that the women were more willing to believe—and to love. Fear and disillusionment had not destroyed them as it had the apostles. "Do not be afraid" Jesus tells them, "Go and carry the news to my brothers." Driven by love they will carry out their apostolate with unbounded enthusiasm, as we will see in the gospels of the rest of this week.

I wonder if there are not two wrong attitudes possible with regard to the resurrection of Jesus. The first is illustrated by the decision of the chief priests in today's gospel to bribe the soldiers to report that the disciples stole Christ's body while they, the soldiers, were asleep: they want *to explain away* the resurrection. The other wrong attitude is in the conviction of those overzealous and rationally inclined Christians who attempt to prove the resurrection by reason. I am convinced that the resurrection is not a doctrine to be proved, but a truth *to be believed* and to be experienced in our lives now. As Thomas Merton put it: "We are called not only to believe that Christ rose from the dead, thereby proving that he was God: we are called upon to experience the Resurrection in our own lives by entering into this dynamic movement, by following Christ who lives in us" (*He Is Risen,* Argus Communications 8).

> The Lord has risen from the dead, as he foretold. Let there be happiness and rejoicing for he is our King for ever (Entrance Antiphon).

But how do we experience the resurrection, how does it give new meaning to our lives now? This was the problem of the people of Jerusalem to whom Peter spoke on that first Pentecost, and we shall see in future readings how they came to find an answer. For now we can say that at least part of the answer was *conversion,* wholehearted conversion to Christ and his way. And if that was good enough for them, it should be good enough for us.

Is it surprising that we speak of conversion now at Easter, after all the emphasis on it during Lent? It should not be, for now, better than then, we see the effects of conversion. Conversion to Jesus is a never ending experience of the Christian, as today's Opening Prayer indicates:

> Help us put into action in our lives
> the baptism we have received with faith.

But Paul tells us in Rom 6 that through baptism we die with Christ by dying to self in order to rise and live with him.

The resurrection was a new beginning for Jesus: his life in this new, resurrected body of his is no longer constrained by the former limitations of space, matter, or time. It surely was a new beginning for the apostles, as we shall see in the weeks ahead. How different their lives after the resurrection and especially after Christ sends them the Holy Spirit from the naive, misinformed thinking, speaking, and acting they manifested before Jesus died! That difference gives us a real insight into the nature of conversion.

The experience of our lenten dying to self and above all our celebration of the Lord's resurrection cannot, may not, leave us unchanged. It has to have made a difference. Easter has to be a new beginning for us all, and it will be if we allow Christ's mind, his love, and his guidance to become essential elements in our daily thinking and living.

There is nothing spectacular about the new life the resurrection summons us to lead. We have heard it before, but now it makes sense. Merton tells us that we should simply follow Christ who now lives in us: "This life, this dynamism, is expressed by the power of love and of encounter: Christ lives in us if we love one another" (*Ibid* 8). Christ lives in us and leads us into a new future which we build together with and for one another.

How appropriate is the Prayer after Communion with which we end today's Mass:

> Lord,
> may the life we receive in these Easter sacraments
> continue to grow in our hearts.
> As you lead us along the way of eternal salvation,
> make us worthy of your many gifts.
>
> Father, you will show me the path to life,
> fullness of joys in your presence,
> the delights at your right hand forever. Alleluia (Responsorial Psalm).

262 TUESDAY OF THE OCTAVE OF EASTER

READING I Acts 2:36-41
GOSPEL John 20:11-18

Reading I: Covers the aftermath of Peter's first sermon, the conversion and baptism of some three thousand of his hearers.
Gospel: Jesus appears to Mary Magdalen, calls her by name, is recognized by her, and sends her to bring the good news of his resurrection to the apostles.

> Father,
> by this Easter mystery you touch our lives with the healing power of your love. . . . May we who now celebrate your gift
> find joy in it for ever in heaven (Opening Prayer).

What a magnificent summary of what Easter is all about! All love heals, but when it is divine love that is in question, there is no limit to its healing power. And that is the kind of love that pours forth from the Easter mystery we are now celebrating. If our lives have not been touched and healed, or if we fall back into spiritual illness and bewilderment, it is no fault of God's, since he gives us the very freedom of his own children. May we always exercise that freedom in choosing deliberately to submit to being loved by our God!

I have long wondered about the persuasive power of Peter's first sermon on Pentecost after he and Our Lady and the apostles received the Holy Spirit. Peter does not argue, does not appeal to reason, does not threaten. He simply relates the events of Christ's life: his miracles, his preaching, his crucifixion and death, followed by his resurrection. Today he concludes the sermon: "Let the whole house of Israel know beyond any doubt that God has made both Lord and Messiah this Jesus whom you crucified" (Reading I).

The sermon resulted in three thousand conversions. How, why? I do not recall that any sermon of Jesus during his lifetime had any such results. Is this a sample of the healing power of God's love? Is it that there is divine power and grace in the very telling of what Jesus was, said, and did? Maybe it is not necessary for me to know the why or the how of the effectiveness of that sermon but simply to rejoice in it and give God thanks for his great glory and mercy.

The death of her beloved Jesus could not quench the love of Mary Magdalen. Now it is even more intense. She is one of the first persons to whom Jesus appears, but strangely she does not immediately recognize him. But she is not the only one not to recognize him. Christ's most intimate friends, men and women alike, mistake him for someone else when they first see him. I can settle for the explanation of some theologians, that there is a newness about him. "He is no longer simply what he was before" (*A New Catechism*, 183). His presence is real, but it is a new presence, and it is no longer subject to any limitations of space, time, or matter. Jesus lives! That is all that matters.

But back to Mary Magdalen. He says only one word, he pronounces her name, and she knows him! How extraordinary! But maybe not. When someone pronounces your name with love, then you know him or her, and you know yourself as you never did before. We find ourselves, as Mary did, in the way Jesus calls us by name.

Mary wants to respond to his love with an embrace, but Jesus gives her a better way. "Go to my brothers," he asks, "and tell them, 'I am ascending to my Father and your Father, to my God and your God.'" And Mary obeys. Like the women in yesterday's gospel, she too becomes an apostle to the apostles. "I have seen the Lord!" she cries out, and they believe her. She brings faith to them and them to the faith—all because she knew how to love and to accept love.

There is one last thought before we leave today's lovely Mass. The Communion Antiphon from Paul's letter to the Colossians instructs us:

> If you have been raised with Christ, seek the things that are above, where Christ is seated at the right hand of God.

I do not believe that Paul wants us to stroll around in a dream as though we were afraid to look life in the eye. I am convinced that it is possible for us to find Christ and enter into a deep intimacy with him in and through our daily life, our work, and above all, our suffering.

I suspect Paul is telling us that we ought to see our whole life as reoriented to Jesus, that we ought to make an ever growing effort to put on his values, his mind. This may well be implicit in the Prayer over the Gifts:

> Lord . . . . May we hold fast to the life you have given us
> and come to the eternal gifts you promise.

He has given us a share in Christ's risen life, but he has also given us life in this world. May he help us to live it to the fullest, in the spirit of our Lord and Savior Jesus Christ!

263 WEDNESDAY OF THE OCTAVE OF EASTER

READING I Acts 3:1-10
GOSPEL Luke 24:13-35

Reading I: Peter and John heal a crippled beggar simply by invoking the name of Jesus.

Gospel: Jesus explains the Scriptures to two disciples on their way to Emmaus, but they recognize him only when he blesses and breaks bread.

Christ's words in today's Entrance Antiphon were originally addressed to those people who cared for and were kind to the poor, the homeless, the starving, and the underprivileged. Today the Church uses this beautiful invitation as a special greeting to the catechumens who were baptized on Holy Saturday night. Of course they can be applied to all who are baptized, whether we were baptized at the Easter Vigil or long ago.

> Come, you whom my Father has blessed; inherit the kingdom prepared for you since the foundation of the world, alleluia.

The best way to keep our "blessedness" alive is to show charity and love to all who are in need.

I find it interesting that the word joy appears three times in today's Opening Prayer:

> God our Father,
> on this solemn feast you give us *the joy of recalling the rising of Christ to new life.*
> May the *joy of our annual celebration*
> bring us to *the joy of eternal life* (italics mine).

Obviously, there are not three kinds of joy; they are all interrelated. The joy of recalling Jesus' rising finds its rich flowering in the celebration of that rising, for the celebration makes that rising present in our midst, and it is all a preview and a foretaste of the unending joy of life with God forever. Alleluia!

Reading I wonderfully illustrates and dramatizes the power of the risen Jesus flowing through the faith filled words of Peter and John. "In the name of Jesus Christ the Nazorean, walk!" Peter commands, and the crippled beggar gladly obeys. His first tentative steps give way to jumps and the praise of God. The Psalmist's words today belong both in the beggar's mouth and in ours:

> Give thanks to the Lord . . . .
> Sing to him, sing his praise,
> proclaim all his wondrous deeds (Responsorial Psalm).

Today's gospel is surely one of the most beloved incidents of the Easter season. The reason we all like it may be that it is so easy for us to identify with these two bewildered disciples. Like them we so often have difficulty understanding the true nature and mission of the Messiah. Above all it is hard for us to understand why we have to follow along the way of the Cross before entering into our glory. How human and how easy to make our own their pleading: "Stay with us. It is nearly evening—the day is practically over." "Stay with us"; this is a prayer rising out of the inmost heart of humanity.

How does Jesus respond to their prayer? He sits down at table with them, takes bread, blesses, breaks it, and hands it to them. Immediately their eyes are opened and they recognize him. The whole affair is wonderfully Eucharistic. He vanishes from their sight, and they react with a beautiful and exact description of the true nature of prayer: "Were not our hearts burning inside us as he talked to us on the road and explained the Scriptures to us?" Jesus talks and their hearts burn. Burning hearts are praying hearts.

How very much we all need Jesus' reminder: "How slow you are to believe all that the prophets have announced! Did not the Messiah have to undergo all this so as to enter into his glory?" The point is, if he had to undergo all that, can we expect to get by without it?

I want to come back to those burning hearts. The burning hearts of the disciples preceded understanding and then recognition. Is not that often the case with us? "The heart has its reasons that the reason does not understand," says Pascal. I suspect that even though we do not have Jesus in person reading and explaining the Scriptures to us, we can have the same kind of satisfying, comforting, and heartwarming experience as those two disciples if we listen to or read the Word of God with faith, with hunger, and with desire.

Finally is there any need for us to be reminded that what we do at every Mass is every bit as realistic and dramatic as this incident? At Mass the same Jesus appears to us and speaks to us every day. He may not explain the inspired words as clearly as he did on the Emmaus road that day; he leaves that to our personal study and the zeal of his priests. But after the readings in the Mass, something takes place that is far more important than that meal in the inn at Emmaus. At the Mass Jesus makes the Last Supper and his sacrifice on Calvary *present for us.* Surely that is more than the two disciples had that day as they walked along and came to the inn.

> The disciples recognized the Lord Jesus in the breaking of bread, alleluia (Communion Antiphon).

With a little fire in our hearts, we can do the same!

THURSDAY OF THE OCTAVE OF EASTER

READING I Acts 3:11-26
GOSPEL Luke 24:35-48

Reading I: Following his cure of the lame man, Peter attributes it all to Jesus, who, he claims, fulfills all the messianic prophecies of Scripture.

Gospel: Jesus appears to his apostles, proves his reality by eating a piece of fish, and then explains how Scripture foretold his death and resurrection.

Both readings today continue events left unfinished in yesterday's readings. The gospel tells of the two disciples' return from Emmaus with the glorious news of Christ's walking with them, explaining the Scriptures to them, and then their coming to know him in the breaking of bread.

Peter draws conclusions from the miracle he worked on the lame cripple, and he takes advantage of the occasion to preach another sermon on the meaning of the Scripture they all knew so well. Or did they know it? If they had, they would have understood how Jesus fulfilled all the prophecies that had been made of him: "God has brought to fulfillment . . . what he announced long ago through the prophets: that his Messiah would suffer."

What is remarkable is that Peter simply imitated what Jesus had said and done during his ministry as stated in today's gospel: "Thus it is written," Jesus says, "that the Messiah must suffer and rise from the dead on the third day. In his name, penance for the remission of sins is to be preached to all the nations."

Like most of his fellow countrymen, Peter had never understood all this. But we may not forget that the sermon recorded in today's reading takes place after his mind had been opened by the Holy Spirit on Pentecost. Now he can spell out in detail the conclusions implicit in what Jesus had said that evening in the Upper Room (gospel). It is the same message of the prophets of old, the message of Jesus' preaching, the message that will remain necessary in all ages to come, ours included: "Reform your lives! Turn to God, that your sins may be wiped away!"

The Church's reaction to all this is marvellously expressed in the Responsorial Psalm:

> O Lord, our Lord,
> how glorious is your name over all the earth!

Jesus rises from the dead, and the Church sees that glorious happening reflected not only in the hearts of Christians but in all the earth, in all creation. The psalm goes on to describe the glorious dignity of the human person:

> You have made him little less than the angels,
> and crowned him with glory and honor.

Is it any wonder that God would want to save us, despite the fact that we have so often refused to remember his lordship over us? But God loves us; he forgives us; he never gives up on anyone. That is what Jesus and his life climaxed by his death and resurrection really tells us: God loves us, and he wants us to return to him and never leave him again.

But there is more to this Mass text that can help us understand the mind of our God. The original "fall of man" is recounted in several incidents described in Genesis. Adam and Eve refused to remember their total dependence on God; they wanted to be like him. But much the same human rebellion is related in the story of the Tower of Babel. Those people wanted to build a tower reaching up to God. The confusion of tongues that resulted is but a mild way of describing the divisiveness among peoples, whether they be nations, or churches, or members of the same.

This is the background of our Opening Prayer today:

> Father,
> you gather the nations to praise your name.
> May all who are reborn in baptism
> be one in faith and love.

It is obvious that this goal of unity among all peoples is far from being fulfilled, but it is not God's fault. Part of our dignity resulting from baptism has to express itself in working for this goal: that we may all some day become one in faith and love and mutual respect.

Peter says in the Communion Antiphon:

> You are a people God claims as his own, to praise him who called you out of darkness into his marvelous light, alleluia.

The best way for all of us to be worthy of that great dignity is to work, to pray, to suffer, even to die that Christ's prayer that all may be one might be granted.

FRIDAY OF THE OCTAVE OF EASTER

READING I Acts 4:1-12
GOSPEL John 21:1-14

Reading I: Peter continues to attribute the cure of the lame man to Jesus.

Gospel: This contains John's account of the return of Jesus and the apostles to the Sea of Tiberias, the miraculous catch of fish, and the meal of fish and bread Jesus prepares for his loved ones.

Jesus and Peter continue to dominate our readings today. It is Friday, and we may well contrast the Jesus of last Friday in agony on the cross with the risen Jesus in a fascinating appearance on the shores of his beloved lake. Then we have the contrast between the fear-driven, cowardly Peter of last Friday and the love-impelled Peter back at his old trade on that same lake.

But perhaps the real contrast is between both of these Peters and the one some fifty days hence, now filled with the Holy Spirit, fearlessly confronting the enemies of Jesus and giving them a lesson in theology: "In the power of that name [Jesus] this man [the cripple] stands before you perfectly sound. This Jesus is 'the stone rejected by you the builders which has become the cornerstone.' There is no salvation in anyone else."

There is a phrase in today's Opening Prayer that accurately describes the new Peter:

> May the new birth we celebrate
> *show its effects in the way we live* (italics mine).

Peter's celebration of the resurrection differs considerably from ours (think of the scene in today's gospel), but the effect in his life is unmistakable. Now he is really an apostle who preaches Christ Jesus and defends him and his way of life at the risk of his own life. The teachings of Jesus—the apostles' "Scripture professor"—which had long remained dormant in Peter's memory now teem with meaning, conviction, and effectiveness.

But back to the gospel. The apostles have left Jerusalem and returned to their old familiar surroundings, the Sea of Tiberias. It is a perfectly natural move after all the emotional turmoil of the past few weeks. Perfectly natural too is Peter's sudden impulsive "I am going out to fish," and his companions' eager "We will join you." The luckless night must have brought back memories of the old days before Jesus found them.

Then comes that same voice again, the voice that had so dramatically changed their lives three years ago: "Children, have you caught anything to eat?" Then, "Cast your net off to the starboard side, . . .

and you will find something." The resulting great catch of fish could mean only one thing. "It is the Lord!" cries the beloved disciple, and you wonder why they did not recognize the voice immediately, before the miraculous catch.

Peter gets so excited he becomes a little irrational. Obviously he wants to get to Jesus as soon as possible and thinks the boat would be too slow. He is stripped, and therefore best equipped for swimming, but he puts on his clothes and then swims to Jesus.

When they all finally get to shore along with their great catch of fish, they see Jesus standing over a fire broiling a fish for them. He invites them: "Come and eat your meal." They obey. Even though he serves them bread, it is obviously not the Eucharist. But there is something Eucharistic about it. It is a meal *served by Jesus* in his role as priest and servant, and they eat and are filled. Never before or since has there ever been a "cookout" like this!

But if you really want to have the full enjoyment of this dearest of Christ's appearances, you have to read the verses following today's incident in the same chapter of John's Gospel when Jesus asks Peter three times: "Simon, son of John, do you love me?" Twice Peter responds: "Yes, Lord, you know that I love you." But the third time the agonizingly repentant apostle cries out: "Lord, you know everything. You know well that I love you." And Jesus confirms Peter, this sinner who had denied him three times, as head of his Church.

Today's Reading I proves how right Jesus was. Lord Jesus, "[Your] kindness endures forever" (Responsorial Psalm).

266 SATURDAY OF THE OCTAVE OF EASTER

READING I Acts 4:13-21
GOSPEL Mark 16:9-15

Reading I: The Leaders, astonished at the change in the apostles, forbid them to preach any more. Peter tells them he would rather obey God.

Gospel: Mark reviews the appearances of Jesus, who, after scolding the apostles for their lack of faith, sends them into the world to "proclaim the good news to all creation."

The Lord led his people to freedom and they shouted with joy and gladness, alleluia (Entrance Antiphon).

The idea of freedom best expresses the meaning of all that Jesus did for us in coming to this world, in suffering, dying, and rising for us. He delivered humankind from slavery to self and to sin and opened up to all a new life characterized by the freedom of the children of God. And it is the Lord, and he alone, who has done this. Only he could have done it, and so we cry:

I will give thanks to you, for you
have answered me. Give thanks to the Lord, for he is good,
for his mercy endures forever (Responsorial Psalm).

This is the sentiment of the catechumens who were baptized a week ago tonight; it is the sentiment of all humanity; it is our own as members of his Church.

The right hand of the Lord has struck with power!
I shall not die, but live, and declare the works of the Lord.

But even though we are redeemed, we need help in order to remain redeemed. Today's Opening Prayer could not be more to the point:

Father of love,
by the outpouring of your grace
you increase the number of those who believe in you.
Watch over your chosen family.
Give undying life to all
who have been born again in baptism.

At the end of this great week of celebrating, the gospel fittingly sums up and reviews the appearances of the risen Jesus for our grateful remembering. We are told that he first appeared to Mary Magdalen, and that she hurried to bring the good news to the apostles. Then the two disciples on the road to Emmaus were favored, and they too felt compelled to hurry to inform the apostles. Finally he appeared to that group itself, and Mark tells us that Jesus took them to task for "their disbelief and their stubbornness" in failing to put faith in his chosen messengers.

But those human faults did not prevent Jesus from commissioning these same apostles to go out and "proclaim the good news to all creation." And why not? For three years he has been preparing them for this moment. Despite their human weaknesses, he believes in them (maybe more than they believe in themselves). For three years he has been preparing them to become the Church, his very own Body, his new presence in which he would continue to live and preach and heal through all ages to come.

So what Jesus says and does today is crucial for understanding him and his life's work. There are many followers of Jesus today who would like to possess and glory in the risen Jesus, but they see no need for the Church, which was the object of all his preaching. What he is really telling us is that you cannot have him without the Church— that frail, weak, vulnerable, doubting, human Church so exactly characterized by this original group who made it up in the beginning.

The first reading justifies Christ's confidence in his chosen ones. It is now after Pentecost and the fulfillment of the promise of the Spirit Jesus had given them while still with them. Peter and John are face-to-face with the very group of dignitaries from whom they had fled in terror only a few days ago. Now it is that same group who are confused and bewildered. They command the apostles to stop mentioning the name of Jesus again. Peter tells them where to get off at: "Judge for yourselves whether it is right in God's sight for us to obey you rather than God."

There would be no Christianity today, there would be no Jesus to believe in and fall in love with, if the apostles had not obeyed his command to go out and preach the good news to all creation. There would be no Easter to celebrate; there would be no joy in the world.

44 SECOND SUNDAY OF EASTER Cycle A

READING I Acts 2:42-47   READING II 1 Pet 1:3-9
GOSPEL   John 20:19-31

Reading I: Contains a description of the life of the first Christians after Pentecost—common sharing of property, eating and breaking bread together.

Reading II: Peter relates Christian baptism to Jesus' resurrection and warns the new Christians to expect suffering and persecution for their faith.

Gospel: Tells of Christ's first appearance to the apostles after the resurrection. He gives them the Holy Spirit. Thomas refuses to believe until Jesus appears again eight days later.

It may be unrealistic to expect the joy and even excitement of Easter to last indefinitely. We can compare the way we felt last week at this time and the letdown we experience today, a week later. We may wonder if we have really experienced Easter, or if it is simply expecting too much of human nature to live constantly on an emotionally high level. There is always danger that religious customs, rituals, and conventions become more real to us than the risen Christ.

Today may be a good day to think back to the Lent we have just finished and to evaluate how well this year's Lent has helped us to know Jesus more intimately. How close, for example, does our thinking come to that of St. Paul when he wrote to the Philippians: "I have come to rate all as loss in the light of the surpassing knowledge of my Lord Jesus Christ. For his sake I have forfeited everything; I have accounted all else rubbish so that Christ may be my wealth and I may be in him. . . . The justice I possess is that which comes through faith in Christ. . . . I wish *to know Christ* and *the power flowing from his resurrection;* likewise to know how to share in his sufferings by being formed in the pattern of his death. Thus do I hope that I may arrive at resurrection from the dead" (italics mine) (Phil 3:8-11).

"To know Christ and the power flowing from his resurrection . . .": this is what Lent and Easter are all about, and this is what life after Easter is about. And for that ongoing knowledge we do not need to remain on a high emotional level. What is essential is faith in Jesus and in his resurrection. This is the chief lesson of the high point of today's Mass, the gospel. It was not Jesus' intention to confound Thomas and make him feel cheap. He had us in mind.

> You became a believer because you saw me.
> Blest are they *who have not seen and have believed* (italics mine).

Many years later the evangelist writes: "These [things] have been recorded to help you believe that Jesus is the Messiah, the Son of God, so that through this faith you might have life in his name." Those words are for us.

The early Christians had that kind of faith in the power of the resurrection and in the living presence of Jesus in their midst. Reading I presents a beautiful picture of how they lived out their faith; they were devoted to the apostles' teaching and the communal life, to the breaking of bread and the prayers. Those who believed shared all things in common, and together they went to the temple area to pray, while in their homes they broke bread and had their meals in common. The result of this kind of life seemed so attractive to non-Christians that day by day they sought to be admitted to the community.

No one would hope or want to duplicate that kind of Christian living today for modern Catholics. But perhaps the essence of the life is possible, namely, faith in Jesus' resurrection and the fact that his concern was for a people more than for individuals.

Today's Alternate Opening Prayer brings the meaning of the life of the early Christians up to date:

> Heavenly Father and God of mercy,
> we no longer look for Jesus among the dead,
> for he is alive and has become the Lord of life.
> From the waters of death you raise us with him
> and renew your gift of life within us.
> Increase in our minds and hearts
> the risen life we share with Christ
> and help us to grow as your people
> toward the fullness of eternal life with you.

I have written elsewhere that we are an Easter people and "Alleluia" is our song. "Alleluia" means "Praise the Lord," and an "Easter people" is a people who, though they have never seen Jesus, love him, believe in him, and rejoice because he has loved them so much that he died and rose from the dead in order to live with them forever. Our Prayer after Communion could not be more to the point:

> Almighty God,
> may the Easter sacraments we have received
> live for ever in our minds and hearts.

May we always

> Give thanks to the Lord, for he is good,
> for his mercy endures forever (Responsorial Psalm).

45 SECOND SUNDAY OF EASTER Cycle B

READING I Acts 4:32-35   READING II 1 John 5:1-6
GOSPEL John 20:19-31

Reading I: Contains a description of the first community of believers in Jesus, their common sharing of possessions, and care for all those in need.

Reading II: John tells us that we can overcome the world because of our faith in Jesus, which makes us God's own children.

Gospel: Relates the dramatic account of Jesus' first appearance to his apostles, Thomas' unbelief, and eight days later his poignant profession of faith: MY LORD AND MY GOD!

Today's gospel is so dramatic that it might possibly distract us from the deep spiritual meaning of the other readings and prayers. Take for example Reading I which relates the results of the apostles' preaching after the first Pentecost. Instinctively, or more exactly providentially, the newly converted Christians gather into a community to which they turn over all their possessions. They demonstrate their faith by caring for the needs of all the community members, and, we can be sure, the needs of nonmembers as well. It is a community possessed of "one heart and one mind," the heart and mind of Jesus himself. This represents a Christian ideal that continues to challenge Christian parishes and religious communities to this day.

Reading II indicates that everything the Christian does derives from a living faith in Jesus as Son of God. Faith in Jesus makes us God's own children, a condition that imposes one main obligation upon us, that of love for the Father demonstrated by caring for the needs of others.

Then there is the gospel. Quite naturally we tend to concentrate on the encounter between Jesus and doubting Thomas. But the gospel should be considered in its entirety. The frightened apostles have locked themselves into their hiding place; suddenly Jesus appears and says: "Peace be with you." He shows them his hands and side and repeats: "Peace be with you." He commissions them to carry on his work after breathing upon them (the ancient sign of the conferring of the Holy Spirit) and says:

> Receive the Holy Spirit.
> If you forgive men's sins,
> they are forgiven them.

He commissions them to carry on his own work.

Do we ever reflect on what brought Jesus to this fear stricken group besides his determination to empower them to carry on his work? He loved these companions of his; he understood their weaknesses, their clouded minds, and their fears. In his compassion he breaks through the locked doors, through their isolation and fear: "Shalom! Peace!" His concern, his compassionate love cannot be locked out.

Now we are ready to reflect on the meaning of his words: "Receive the Holy Spirit." Become new beings, become a new people, a people capable of rising out of fear, a courageous people, capable of any adventure, any hardship, capable of bearing witness to your newfound faith even to the point of martyrdom and death. Receive the Holy Spirit, the Spirit of love, the Spirit of *enthusiasm*—of being possessed by God—forgive sins. Do all that I have done. Preach reconciliation and peace between people and their God, between peoples who are divided. Preach the peace I am bestowing upon you.

Only then does the Thomas incident take place, and we can be forever grateful to dear doubting Thomas for demonstrating in word and deed that real faith is not *primarily* assenting to truths and doctrines but that it is surrendering one's whole life and future to the Person Jesus in total loving trust and total self-abandonment.

This gospel incident is timeless, it is ever new. Our life as Christians in the modern Church in whatever vocation is often like that of the apostles in that upper room. Fear, doubt, worry about the future of the Church, the country, the family, the religious community, to say nothing of our own personal future in this world and the next, may have caused us to lock all doors and darken all windows.

Today Jesus appears to us and says: Shalom! Peace! Receive the Holy Spirit. Carry on my work. Be a community, a family, a parish of one heart and one mind, *my* heart, *my* mind. Be reconcilers, be at peace, make peace, and let the joy of my victory over fear, death, and sin flood your hearts. Forgive and you shall be forgiven. In a word, *believe.* Give me your heart, your mind. Do you not realize that it was you I was thinking of when I said to Thomas:

> You became a believer because you saw me.
> Blest are they *who have not seen and have believed (italics mine)?*

There can be only one answer to such a profession of divine love and confidence in us: "My Lord and my God!" With that confession in the back of our minds and in our hearts, everything is possible for us. We can cast out old fears and anxieties, hesitations and prejudices and be ready for whatever life might bring.

We can say amen to this meditation with one of the best Alternate Opening Prayers of the year:

> Heavenly Father and God of mercy,
> we no longer look for Jesus among the dead,

for he is alive and has become the Lord of life.
From the waters of death you raise us with him
and renew your gift of life within us.
Increase in our minds and hearts
the risen life we share with Christ
and *help us to grow as your people
toward the fullness of eternal life with you.*
We ask this through Christ our Lord (italics mine).
Amen.

46   SECOND SUNDAY OF EASTER   Cycle C

READING I   Acts 5:12-16   **READING II**   Rev 1:9-11, 12-13, 17-19
GOSPEL   John 20:19-31

Reading I: This gives an early account of the miracles and signs worked by the apostles after they had received the Holy Spirit.

Reading II: On the island of Patmos, the Apostle John has a vision of Jesus in glory, and he receives the command to write down his visions.

Gospel: Contains the dramatic account of Jesus' first appearance to the apostles, his bestowing the Holy Spirit upon them, and the dramatic account of Thomas' profession of faith after his initial doubt.

Today's Mass might be labelled a Mass of echoes. The echoes are, of course, of Jesus' death and resurrection (gospel), of baptism with its new beginnings (Entrance Antiphon, Opening Prayer), and of the beginnings of Christianity after the apostles had received the Holy Spirit on Pentecost. But unlike the echoes we sometimes experience, which are so momentary and passing, the echoes of this Mass have a lasting reality, or they could have if we back them up with some personal response, particularly a response of grateful, lasting joy.

There is no scientific proof that Jesus rose from the dead. We simply believe. Jesus had all future generations in mind when he said to Thomas:

> You became a believer because you saw me.
> Blest are they who have not seen and have believed.

So there may be no scientific proof, but what could be more convincing than the observable presence of Christ in the lives of Christians?

There are several ways of manifesting the presence of the risen Jesus in our lives, not least of which is a constant attitude of quiet joy. This may come as a surprise to many Catholics, especially in these days when the very existence of human life is so threatened. Long, sad faces are probably more in evidence than joyous confident ones. Commentators and preachers love to quote the destructive atheist, Nietzsche: "If you Christians expect me to believe in your God, you'll have to learn how to sing better songs, you'll have to learn *how to look more redeemed*" (italics mine).

To be sure, joy need not be loud or boisterously manifested. There is also a quiet joy that is authentic and that can exist in hearts overflowing with love, even when those hearts are overwhelmed with sorrow and pain.

> Rejoice to the full in the glory that is yours, and give thanks to God who called you to his kingdom, alleluia (Alternative Entrance Antiphon).

There is another way of manifesting the presence of the risen Jesus in our lives. In the gospel Jesus says to his apostles:

> Receive the Holy Spirit.
> If you forgive men's sins,
> they are forgiven them;
> if you hold them bound,
> they are held bound.

We Catholics rightly believe that Jesus was here conferring on the apostles and their successors the same power to forgive sins that he possessed. But there may be a broader interpretation that applies to all the baptized: we can show forth our belief in the risen Christ and make that presence manifest when we exercise the spirit of forgiveness and reconciliation contained in his words to us: "Peace be with you . . . forgive one another as I have forgiven you."

When we seek and strive for reconciliation, when we genuinely care for one another and try to understand one another's problems, Christ is present in us and in those we minister to. The resurrection becomes a reality in our lives instead of being only an echo.

Today's Alternate Opening Prayer may well summarize all that the resurrection can and ought to mean in our lives, also the secret for maintaining the presence of the risen Jesus in our attitudes:

> From the waters of death you raise us with him
> and renew your gift of life within us.
> Increase in our minds and hearts
> the risen life we share with Christ and help us to grow as your people
> toward the fullness of eternal life with you.

So do not be afraid. "There is nothing to fear. I am the First and the Last and the One who lives. Once I was dead but now I live—forever and ever" (Reading II).

With such an assurance from Jesus himself, we can surely

> Give thanks to the Lord for he is good,
> for his mercy endures forever (Responsorial Psalm).

267 MONDAY OF THE SECOND WEEK OF EASTER

READING I Acts 4:23-31
GOSPEL John 3:1-8

Reading I: When Peter and John are released from prison, their small community, inspired by the Holy Spirit, breaks into prayer.

Gospel: At the beginning of his ministry, Jesus explains to Nicodemus how he must be born again of water and the Spirit in order to enter the kingdom.

On hearing the prayers and readings of today's Mass, one might almost think we are celebrating Pentecost rather than Easter. The truth is that historically the Jewish Passover and Pentecost belonged together. The liberation of the Jews from slavery in Egypt at the Exodus was followed fifty days later by the giving of the Law and the foundation of the covenant between God and his people on Mt. Sinai. That event was celebrated in their feast of Pentecost.

Again historically the Christian Easter and the Christian Pentecost also belong together. Easter would have been inconceivable without the coming of the Holy Spirit upon the Church. During his lifetime Jesus preached, worked signs, healed, forgave sins, formed the apostles into a Church, and promised to send the Holy Spirit to that Church. He suffered, died, and was buried. He rose from the dead, and we celebrated that glorious event only eight days ago. Fifty days after he rose from the dead, *on the Jewish feast of Pentecost,* Jesus fulfilled his promise and sent the Spirit upon the apostles, and they became his Church, his Body, his new presence in the world. In this new presence he proposed to live, work, heal—in a word to continue to do all that he has done in his physical presence in Palestine. It was the Holy Spirit who made a living organism out of the organization that Jesus had prepared by his three years of preaching to and educating the apostles.

We have heard this past week how Peter and John were able to function as a result of their having received the Spirit on that first Christian Pentecost. They were transformed, changed, charged up. For the first time they were able to understand the true meaning of what Jesus had been telling them for three years. Their former fears had given way to courageous and bold proclamation of Jesus' resurrection and to proper condemnation of those who had crucified the Lord.

Today's first reading is an excellent example of the excitement that prevailed in the early Church after the Spirit had fired it up. The members felt involved in the preaching of Peter and John; they understood the old prophecies pertaining to Jesus. They felt threatened by coming persecution, but they were unafraid, for they had confidence that the Lord would hear their prayer. And what a prayer! It literally shook the place where they were praying, and the answer was a kind of mini-Pentecost: "They were filled with the Holy Spirit and continued to speak God's word with confidence."

We are members of that same Church preached by the apostles and founded on them with Jesus himself as the chief cornerstone. The message of that Church today is that just as the Holy Spirit was necessary to complete the work of Christ in his time, so is that same Spirit necessary to complete the Easter dying and rising in us and in our lives now. For fervor can grow cold, understanding can fade, intimacy can vanish. So we pray:

> Almighty and ever-living God,
> your Spirit made us your children,
> confident to call you Father.
> Increase your Spirit of love within us
> and bring us to our promised inheritance (Opening Prayer).

No one has ever claimed that a person is once and for all converted to Christ. Conversion is an ongoing, never-ending dynamic process, one that can easily be interrupted and even destroyed. It is the Holy Spirit who inspires that process of conversion and gives it new inspiration and vitality. It is the Holy Spirit finally who changes us from mere professed followers of Christ into mature, enthusiastic adults in the faith.

It is this conversion that Jesus is talking about in the gospel:

> no one can enter into God's kingdom
> without being begotten of water and Spirit.
> Flesh begets flesh,
> Spirit begets spirit.
> Do not be surprised that I tell you
> you must all be begotten from above.

> The wind blows where it will. . . .
> So it is with everyone begotten of the Spirit.

We can only pray: "Father, increase your Spirit of love within us" (from the Opening Prayer), and then our lives will bear fruit in more love.

268 TUESDAY OF THE SECOND WEEK OF EASTER

READING I Acts 4:32-37
GOSPEL John 3:7-15

Reading I: Contains a description of the communal life of the first Christians and the popular favorable reaction to this life.

Gospel: This passage is a continuation of the conversation between Jesus and Nicodemus and Jesus' prophecy that he will be "lifted up" like the brazen serpent.

We will be hearing and pondering John's Gospel from now until Pentecost, which means that we will be receiving John's special insights into the nature of the sacraments of baptism and the Eucharist, thus preparing ourselves for the coming of the Holy Spirit upon us at Pentecost.

In today's gospel we receive instruction, not only about our spiritual rebirth in baptism but also about the ongoing conversion that must characterize every Christian's postbaptismal life as a member of the Church. This rebirth and ongoing conversion is the work of the Holy Spirit in us now.

Today's gospel reading closes with Jesus comparing himself to the brazen serpent in the Sinai desert (Numbers 21:9). The Jews who looked upon the serpent raised high on a pole were healed of their serpent-inflicted wounds. We who look with burning faith upon Jesus raised on his cross must necessarily enter upon a way of life deliberately oriented to him, a way of life that will surely bring us eventually to share his eternal life. As "Christ had to suffer and rise from the dead, and so enter into his glory" (Communion Antiphon), so must the follower of Christ. There is no other way. The Christian life of continuous conversion involves suffering; it requires dying to self, but eyes fixed on Jesus removes all hesitancy.

As the Gospel of John provides continuous reading for us in the gospels of this Easter season, instructing us in the nature of our sacramental life, so the Acts of the Apostles provides vivid insights into the life of the early Christian community after the first Pentecost. Today we see how the first Christians chose to respond to Christ's love for them by deliberately choosing to live a life of poverty. Members of the community freely chose to relinquish all rights to personal property so that everything was held in common. This was possible because they were of "one heart and one mind," the heart and mind of Christ himself, who, they were convinced, lived in them as the heart and center of their community.

Is it extreme to believe that this oneness of mind and heart and the common possession of goods were what provided the apostles and their converts with the power to bear witness to the resurrection of the Lord? The entire community felt involved in their preaching and felt responsible for its success.

Not many modern Christians choose to give up ownership of property in order to follow Christ, nor does the Church claim it is necessary. But what is necessary is that the communities of believers—our parishes and religious communities—of which we are all members be of one mind and one heart, and that we manifest this unity both in caring for the poor and needy and in giving our best efforts to perfecting and entering joyfully into our community worship.

It may be embarrassing to ask if this ideal of one heart and one mind characterizes our parishes and religious communities today. Do we as individuals have any concern about cultivating that blessed kind of unity? How much enthusiasm can we give to the sentiments contained in our Entrance Antiphon:

> Let us shout out our joy and happiness, and give glory to God, the Lord of all, because he is our King?

If we lack oneness of mind and heart, we really need today's Opening Prayer:

> . . . help us to proclaim the power of the Lord's resurrection.

And we might add: grant us the oneness of mind and heart that comes from seeing the death and resurrection of Jesus as the sign of his love for us.

In each of today's prayers, we plead for eternal life, eternal happiness. The prayers enforce our faith in seeing a continuity between our life in this world and our life in the world to come. The entire Mass confirms our faith that the best preparation for eternal happiness is living fully and joyfully in a community or parish in which there is one heart and one mind: the heart and mind of Jesus our Lord who lives now in us all.

269 WEDNESDAY OF THE SECOND WEEK OF EASTER

READING I Acts 5:17-26
GOSPEL John 3:16-21

Reading I: The high priest and the Sadducees have some of the apostles put in prison, but they are delivered by an angel.

Gospel: Continuation of the dialogue between Jesus and Nicodemus: "God so loved the world that he gave his only Son" for its salvation.

Today's first reading indicates how actively and effectively the Lord worked in and on that first community of Christians in Jerusalem. He had no intention of allowing the spread of the good news of Jesus' resurrection to be limited or stopped by those who had engineered Christ's crucifixion. Once again we see how powerfully transforming was the Holy Spirit in the lives of the apostles. They fearlessly put themselves at the disposal of the Spirit; they belong no longer to themselves but to Christ Jesus.

The Responsorial Psalm reflects how the apostles might have reacted to their deliverance:

> The Lord hears the cry of the poor.
> I will bless the Lord at all times;
> his praise shall be ever in my mouth. . . .
> I sought the Lord, and he answered me
> and delivered me from all my fears.

Now the prayer belongs to us all. There is more than one kind of prison. This is our plea for deliverance from the prison of self-indulgence, pride, self-sufficiency:

> Taste and see how good the Lord is;
> happy the man who takes refuge in him.

There may be something significant in the way the word world appears so often in today's liturgy. In the gospel Jesus tells Nicodemus and us:

> Yes, God so loved the world
> that he gave his only Son,
> that whoever believes in him may not die
> but may have eternal life.
> God did not send the Son into the world
> to condemn the world,
> but that the world might be saved through him.

Martin Luther is supposed to have said that this verse is the entire Gospel in miniature.

I believe it would be a mistake to understand Jesus as referring

33

only to the souls of human beings. He has in mind the whole human person, soul and body, and more than that, the material world as well. After all Genesis tells us how once he had brought the universe into existence "God saw how good it was" (see Gen 1:10ff.). There are some theologians who believe that the world, like its master, the human person, fell with the fall of that master and is also in need of redemption. And God so loved this world that he sent his Son that this world might be saved through him.

But back to the main idea of the gospel: the love that God has for the world in all its meanings. God's love is completely unselfish, so much so that he gives up his dearest possession, his only Son, in order to restore the world and its citizens to loving friendship and intimacy with him. This gospel says so much about God, but so much, too, about ourselves and our worth in the sight of God.

With the gospel statement of God's personal love for us as our common Christian possession, it is difficult to understand how the concept of a "policeman God," forever trying to catch his children in wrongdoing so as to punish them could ever have taken hold on so many Christians. With Jesus himself as the greatest sacrament (sign) of divine love, how was it possible for people to believe more in their often petty sins than in God's loving-kindness? It is tragic for any of us to refuse to believe that we are unworthy of being loved into forgiveness.

One of the greatest lessons we should have learned from our Holy Week Easter experience is the extent of the Father's love for us. Perhaps an even greater lesson is in learning how to accept that love and allow it to convince us to share it with others who have not known it. Jesus surely had this and us in mind when he said:

> I have chosen you from the world to go and bear fruit that will last (Communion Antiphon).

In a word, realizing how much we have been loved will help us want to make our own today's Entrance Antiphon:

> I will be a witness to you in the world, O Lord. I will spread the knowledge of your name among my brothers, alleluia.

> Glorify the Lord with me,
> let us together extol his name (Responsorial Psalm).

270 THURSDAY OF THE SECOND WEEK OF EASTER

READING I   Acts 5:27-33
GOSPEL   John 3:31-36

Reading I: On trial before the high priest and the Sanhedrin, the apostles continue boldly to express their intention to preach the good news.

Gospel: Jesus continues his theology lesson for Nicodemus: "the One whom God has sent speaks the words of God." And Jesus is the one sent.

The liberation of the Jews from slavery in Egypt, their passage through the Red Sea, the journey through the desert to Mount Sinai and eventually to the Promised Land are often seen together as an image of the journey of the Church, the new people of God, through history. It is also the image of the life of the individual Christian.

The main thought is that it is God who delivered the Jews, it is God who walked with them on their way. Today's Entrance Antiphon is a beautiful expression of this firm Jewish conviction:

> When you walked at the head of your people, O God, and lived with them on their journey, the earth shook at your presence, and the skies poured forth their rain, alleluia.

The antiphon now expresses our Christian conviction and belief as well. We too are on a pilgrimage to the Promised Land with God in the lead. If he is with us, who can be against us!

Jesus died and rose from the dead. His death and resurrection have freed us from slavery to sin and to self. The memory of our celebration of his death and resurrection is still vivid and dear. In a few weeks we will celebrate his ascension. But we know he will not leave us, for before he ascended to the Father, he promised:

> I, the Lord, *am with you always*, until the end of the world (Communion Antiphon) (italics mine).

The conclusion for all—for the Church, for our families, parishes, religious communities, and for each of us singly (especially when we become worried about our present and future)—must therefore be, to borrow the words of Fr. Bob Dufford's song: "Be not afraid. I go before you always. Come, follow me, and I will give you rest" (*Glory and Praise* [Phoenix: North American Liturgy Resources] 10). If anyone has ever earned our confidence, it is Jesus, "the One whom God has sent" (gospel) out of sheer, undeserved love for us.

Surely we encounter obstacles and threats from without and from within, as there were for Peter and the infant Church. There is no escaping them. The authorities forbade the apostles to preach about "that name," Jesus. But Peter replied: "Better for us to obey God than men! The God of our fathers has raised up Jesus whom you put to death, hanging him on a tree. He whom God has exalted at his right hand as ruler and savior is to bring repentance to Israel and forgiveness of sins. We testify to this. So too does the Holy Spirit, whom God has given to those that obey him" (Reading I). This is the same Peter who just a few weeks before had denied that he ever knew Jesus! When the Sanhedrin heard Peter's speech, "they were stung to a fury and wanted to kill them" (Reading I), and we shall see in future readings how it all ends.

For the time being, and reflecting and relying upon God's promises to his people and to us, we can make our own today's Responsorial Psalm:

> The Lord hears the cry of the poor.
> I will bless the Lord at all times;
> his praise shall be ever in my mouth.
> Taste and see how good the Lord is;
> happy the man who takes refuge in him. . . .
> The Lord is close to the brokenhearted;
> and those who are crushed in spirit he saves.

It is hard to imagine anything more comforting than those last words!

In today's Opening Prayer we cry to our God:

> God of mercy,
> may the Easter mystery we celebrate
> be effective throughout our lives.

There may be many ways for the Easter mystery to be effective in our lives, but it is apparent that the way all of us need most is a deeper faith in and awareness of our risen Savior's being present in and to us, leading us in our pilgrimage of faith on the way to our Promised Land.

> Almighty and ever-living Lord,
> you restored us to life
> by raising Christ from death.
> Strengthen us by this Easter sacrament;
> may we feel its saving power in our daily life (Prayer after Communion).

To that prayer we all cry out, AMEN!

271 FRIDAY OF THE SECOND WEEK OF EASTER

READING I Acts 5:34-42
GOSPEL John 6:1-15

Reading I: The persecuted apostles find a defender in Gamaliel, and they are released but commanded not to preach again. They do not obey.

Gospel: Jesus begins his instruction on the Eucharist by feeding five thousand with five barley loaves and some dried fish, miraculously multiplied.

Two weeks ago today we celebrated the life-giving death of Jesus. With the memory of that day still fresh in our minds and hearts, we are grateful for its echoes in today's Mass:

> By your blood, O Lord, you have redeemed us from every tribe and tongue, from every nation and people: you have made us into the kingdom of God (Entrance Antiphon).

The Communion Antiphon is even more explicit:

> Christ our Lord was put to death for our sins; and he rose again to make us worthy of life, alleluia.

We remember with hearts overflowing with love and gratitude, and we need that remembering, for without it we cease to grow as fervent followers of Christ.

But happy remembering of the past does not prevent us from reflecting on the present and the future. In Reading I we are still in Jerusalem with our ancestors in the Faith who are undergoing their own personal passion, persecution at the hands of the Sanhedrin. But now they have an unexpected defender, Gamaliel, whose inspired counsel in evaluating Christianity is as valid today as it was then: "Let them alone. If their purpose or activity is human in its origins, it will destroy itself. If, on the other hand, it comes from God, you will not be able to destroy them without fighting God himself." Are there movements or "revivals" in the Catholic Church today to which that criterion might apply?

The Sanhedrin had a strange way of accepting Gamaliel's advice. It had the apostles whipped and forbade them to preach Jesus before letting them go. Needless to say, the apostles "never stopped teaching and proclaiming the good news of Jesus the Messiah." And why not, convinced as they were that "The Lord is my light and my salvation; whom should I fear?" (Responsorial Psalm).

It helps to understand these Easter season gospels by recalling that John's Gospel, written at the end of the first century long after the events of Jesus' life took place, is primarily a final instruction for new converts on the nature of the Church, specifically the nature of the sacramental life of the Church. In previous readings this week we have heard Jesus' teaching on the nature of baptismal rebirth through water and the Holy Spirit and the ongoing lifelong conversion baptism demands of the Christian.

Now we come to a kind of prologue to Christ's teaching on the Eucharist, and we see Jesus at his pedagogical best. He teaches by doing, he speaks through a spectacular sign. He took five barley loaves, "gave thanks, and passed them around to those reclining there; he did the same with the dried fish, as much as they wanted." Miraculously multiplied loaves and fishes form an evident sign to the five thousand diners. But it is a sign, not of the king the people wanted him to be but of the world's Savior, aware of a much deeper need all people have—union with him by means of bread and wine become his Body and Blood. Coming gospels will provide us with details.

> Father,
> in your plan of salvation
> your Son Jesus Christ accepted the cross
> and freed us from the power of the enemy.
> May we come to share the glory of his resurrection. . . . (Opening Prayer).

It is obvious that the best way for us to share the glory of the resurrection is by loving participation in that sacrament which today's miracle prefigured, the Eucharist. For it is the Eucharist that makes present for us here and now the *entire life* of Jesus, his preaching, his miracles, and above all, his passion, death, and resurrection. Never was a Responsorial Psalm more appropriate:

> The Lord is my light and my salvation;
> whom should I fear? . . .
> One thing I ask of the Lord;
> this I seek:
> To dwell in the house of the Lord
> all the days of my life,
> That I may gaze on the loveliness of the Lord . . .
> I believe that I shall see the bounty of the Lord
> in the land of the living.

The bounty of the Lord is the Body and Blood of Jesus, Son of God, become our food. Alleluia!

272 SATURDAY OF THE SECOND WEEK OF EASTER

READING I Acts 6:1-7
GOSPEL   John 6:16-21

Reading I: Urged by Greek converts, the apostles decide to ordain helpers to care for the community's daily needs while they continue to preach.

Gospel: After the multiplication of loaves, Jesus walks on the water to his disciples in the boat.

What a wonderful way for us to be greeted when we begin our Mass today:

> You are a people God claims as his own, to praise him who called you out of darkness into his marvelous light, alleluia (Entrance Antiphon).

This is Peter writing to his flock of newly baptized Christians (1 Pet 2:9). He was simply paraphrasing God's own profession of love for and faith in his chosen people: "You are a people sacred to the Lord, your God; he has chosen you from all the nations on the face of the earth to be a people peculiarly his own. It was not because you are the largest of all nations that the Lord set his heart on you and chose you . . . [but] because the Lord loved you" (Deut 7:6-8).

Those words are now addressed to us. This is who we are: chosen by God to exist, chosen by him to be his very own, chosen to praise him who called us out of darkness into his marvellous light. The idea of God's having chosen us in Christ Jesus comes through also in the Communion Antiphon which quotes Jesus himself:

> Father, I want the men you have given me to be with me where I am, so that they may see the glory you have given me. . . .

A people, a flock, needs care, and today's Reading I tells us the practical steps the apostles took to see to the spiritual and physical needs of those early Christians. "It is not right for us to neglect the word of God in order to wait on tables," the Twelve decided, and they told the people to choose men whom they considered worthy of being the apostles' helpers. The apostles commissioned or ordained the men by praying over them and imposing hands on them. This ceremony of praying over candidates for ordination to the diaconate and the priesthood and calling down the Holy Spirit upon them by the laying on of hands continues to be the heart of the ordination ceremony to this day.

In the gospel Jesus continues his "instruction" on the nature of the greatest manifestation of his never-ending care for his flock, the Eucharist. One evident sign of his divine power, the multiplication of loaves, has ended, and now evening is drawing on. We are not told why the disciples decided to cross the lake when it was dark. All we know is that a storm comes up and they become frightened. Then Jesus comes to them, walking on the water. He calms their fears: "It is I; do not be afraid." Before they know it, they are at land. The point is: if Jesus can feed thousands with five loaves and a few fish and if he can walk on water and calm the storm angered waves, what is there that he cannot and will not do?

We may again be reminded that John's Gospel was intended primarily as the final instruction of converts on the Church and its sacraments. We may need this instruction as much as those early Christians. But today's Mass also sees to some of our other needs.

The fear of the apostles is so much like our own. We fear for loved ones; we fear storms, accidents, sickness, even life itself. So our cry today is most appropriate:

> May your kindness, O Lord, be upon us who have put our hope in you (Responsorial Psalm).

This is a cry from the very heart of humankind and from each of us in person. It is a plea that does not go unanswered. Again today Jesus comes to us walking on life's rough waters, and we hear his voice: "It is I; do not be afraid." No matter what the problem, the pain, the worry, that voice will never be stilled.

> But see, the eyes of the Lord are
> upon those who fear him,
> upon those who hope for his kindness,
> To deliver them from death
> and preserve them in spite of famine (Responsorial Psalm).

There is only one response to all the good news of this Mass, and we make it a prayer:

> Lord,
> may this eucharist,
> which we have celebrated in memory of your Son,
> help us to grow in love (Prayer after Communion).

47 THIRD SUNDAY OF EASTER Cycle A

READING I Acts 2:14, 22-28 READING II I Peter 1:17-21
GOSPEL Luke 24:13-35

Reading I: On Pentecost Sunday Peter preaches to the people of Jerusalem, reviewing Jesus' life and works and accusing the people of killing him.

Reading II: Peter tells his people about the results of Christ's death and resurrection: they are "delivered from the futile way of life."

Gospel: This contains Luke's account of the two disciples on the road to Emmaus, how Jesus joins them and explains the Scriptures, and how they recognize him in the breaking of the bread.

Peter's first sermon is quite a performance. We can grasp its drama and meaning better if we recall the background, the history. This is the same Peter who fished on the lake, who followed Jesus for three years and was chosen by him as the first among the apostles, the Peter who denied ever having known Jesus when the latter was on trial, and the Peter who had seen Jesus after his resurrection and had been present at the ascension of the Master. The Peter we meet today is obviously a changed man. The bumbling, impulsive, ignorant, fearful, terribly human Peter of the Gospels now stands before thousands of Jews who had come to celebrate the Jewish feast of Pentecost in Jerusalem and preaches to them, accusing them of having crucified Jesus. He even quotes their familiar prophecy and shows how it is fulfilled in Jesus' resurrection.

If this is the same old Peter we once knew, something has obviously happened to him, and we know what that "something" is. The Holy Spirit, promised by Jesus, has come to the apostles and women in that upper room, has brushed away their ignorance, given them insight into the true meaning of the old prophecies and events of Hebrew history and made them understand that Jesus is the Savior and the deliverer not from Roman oppression but from enslavement to Satan and a "futile way of life." Today's Reading is only the beginning of the sermon; if you are impatient to know how it was received and what its results were, read all of Acts 2.

Peter the preacher becomes Peter the theologian in Reading II: "Realize that you were delivered from the futile way of life your fathers handed on to you . . . by Christ's blood beyond all price. . . . Your faith and hope, then, are *centered in God*" (italics mine).

This is a most unusual observation, especially in the light of modern psychology. People seek and need to find meaning in their lives in this world. A desire for personal fulfillment is planted deep in human hearts. To try to find this fulfillment (and one's own personal identity) apart from the One who created these hearts of ours is futile. The German theologian Helmut Thielicke puts it well: "I obtain freedom to be myself only when I become free for God" *(Being a Christian When the Chips Are Down,* translated by H. George Anderson, Philadelphia: Fortress Press, 1981, 32). When life is no longer centered on God, it becomes futile and meaningless. That is Peter's message.

We could hardly imagine a more fitting introduction to the gospel than today's Gospel Verse:

> Lord Jesus, make your word plain to us,
> make our hearts burn with love when you speak.

Burning hearts are praying hearts, the kind of hearts best fitted for Christians.

The gospel takes us back to that famous walk to Emmaus on the first Easter day. The details are familiar, for it is one of the most precious of all Jesus' appearances. The distressed disciples are joined by a mysterious stranger who explains the Scriptures to them while their hearts burn within them. "Stay with us . . . ," they plead, "the day is practically over." He disappears the moment he breaks bread for them at the meal, and in that breaking of bread they recognize him. Their prayer, "Stay with us," is our prayer now.

Because of his resurrection Jesus is able to answer that plea. He walks through life with us, he explains the Scriptures for us, and best of all he breaks bread with and for us at every Eucharist. Actually we have more than the disciples had that day at Emmaus, for the breaking of bread that we have—the Mass—is the Last Supper and Calvary made present in our midst.

Whether or not our hearts burn within us depends on the openness of those hearts to the deep meanings of the Word, on our willingness to put our lives in his hands, and on our desire for him to fulfill every need of our lives.

> Lord Jesus, . . .
> make our hearts burn with love when you speak.

48 THIRD SUNDAY OF EASTER Cycle B

READING I   Acts 3:13-15, 17-19   READING II   I John 2:1-5
GOSPEL   Luke 24:35-48

Reading I: Peter speaks to the people of Jerusalem, tells them they have acted out of ignorance in killing Jesus, and exhorts them to reform.

Reading II: John states that his purpose in writing is to keep his people from sin, but if they fall again, Jesus will forgive them.

Gospel: Jesus again appears to the apostles, proves he is risen by inviting them to touch him, proves from Scripture that the Messiah had to suffer and urges the preaching of penance to all nations.

If we listen to or read carefully today's readings, we might conclude that their chief emphasis is on sin and the need for conversion. To be sure Peter does accuse his hearers of murdering Christ, the author of life, and John says: "I am writing this to keep you from sin."

But there is something deeper here than mere accusation and incrimination. There is forgiveness, *divine forgiveness*. Peter recognizes this because he himself has experienced the forgiveness of Jesus for his own denial of Christ and in speaking to the people he remembers the scene in today's gospel. So he tells his hearers that they acted out of ignorance. And John says he wants to prevent sin, "But if anyone should sin, we have . . . Jesus Christ, an intercessor who is just," who is constantly working with us to perfect us: "whoever keeps his word, truly has the love of God been made perfect in him."

In the gospel we read Luke's version of Jesus' first appearance to the apostles. They can hardly believe their eyes and think he is a ghost. So he makes elaborate efforts to prove that he is real, that he is risen. He invites them to touch him, he asks for something to eat, and he eats some cooked fish. "Then he opened their minds to the understanding of the Scriptures," telling them that it was written that the Messiah had to suffer and rise from the dead. "In his name, penance for the remission of sins is to be preached to all the nations."

All this is obvious. But that there might be something deeper in the gospel is indicated in Christ's first greeting: "Peace to you. . . . Why are you disturbed?" What does this greeting imply? To understand we have to recall the recent past and how they all, with the exception of John, deserted him while he was being tried and crucified. So Jesus' greeting of "Peace to you" may well mean: "Let your hearts be at rest. Let there be no self-condemnation. YOU ARE FORGIVEN. You are reconciled. You belong to me again. We are friends. Peace to you. I am not going to accuse you. All I want from you from now on is that you remember my forgiveness, turn away from the past, and make a new beginning."

We can be sure the disciples will never forget this personal experience of divine forgiveness. They may falter and even fall again, for they are human, but from now on picking themselves up and returning to Christ, living with him and for him will be easier, for they will always see him standing there that first Easter evening, saying to them: "Peace to you."

That same experience is now ours. We have all probably had enough falls in our life to take deep consolation from the words of Jesus spoken today to us: "Peace to you. . . . Let your hearts be at rest. . . . You belong to me again." The heart of Christian morality may well be in these words of Jesus and our reaction to them. For many people, even for many Christians, morality is obedience to laws and rules. Such obedience is ethics, and one does not have to be a Christian to practice ethics. Morality for the Christian, according to a modern theologian, is rather personal responsiveness to divine love, as was the case with the apostles, as should be the case with us. In Jesus love becomes visible, and the apostles respond; they give in to it.

Jesus recognizes that turning from sin is essential, and we all need such repentance; it may even be an essential condition for forgiveness. But "repentance and forgiveness are two sides of the desire to leave the offending past behind and make a new beginning" (Father Robert Beck, *The Dubuque Witness*, April 14, 1985). I insist that the new beginning is essentially clinging to Christ and growing in him and that it be motivated by an ongoing personal love. Otherwise it will not last.

With all this in mind, it could be that this picture of Jesus standing before us, saying "Peace to you" is the most essential and necessary one for us to have always before us. It will make our hearts burn within us with love for him, and he will have "restored the joy of our youth" (Opening Prayer).

49 THIRD SUNDAY OF EASTER Cycle C

READING I Acts 5:27-32, 40-41 READING II Rev 5:11-14
GOSPEL John 21:1-19

Reading I: When the high priest forbids the apostles to preach about Jesus, they respond: "Better for us to obey God than men!"

Reading II: This relates John's vision of Jesus being acclaimed in heaven by angels: "Worthy is the Lamb that was slain."

Gospel: Jesus prepares breakfast for his apostles on the shore of the Sea of Tiberias, then asks Peter three times: "Do you love me?"

Let all the earth cry out to the Lord with joy; praise the glory of his name; proclaim his glorious praise, alleluia (Entrance Antiphon).

What a marvellous theme song for today's celebration! Our human insufficiency prompts us to enlist the potential praise of all creation as we contemplate the wonders the Lord has done for us in the glorious resurrection of Jesus.

Today's gospel dramatizes what the Lord did in one of the dearest of the resurrection appearances of Jesus. Scholars say that this gospel is kind of a P.S. added by the followers of the evangelist John, but what is wrong with a P.S? When we use one, we simply make a letter more worthy of being read. This incident literally glows with mystery, memories, love, friendship, regret, and promise.

At first—at least for the apostles—memories must predominate. They recall the old days spent on this lake before *he* came into their lives: the first miraculous catch of fish; his invitation to "Come, follow me"; the multiplication of loaves on the shore of this same lake; and then his walking to them "across the liquid plain" to calm their fears as they huddled in their storm tossed boat.

Other memories come back, for instance, the last Passover meal with them when he washed their feet after saying, "With desire have I desired to eat this Passover with you before I suffer." Peter especially remembers his words to Jesus: "I will lay down my life for you." And then he went out and denied him three times. Three times did Peter swear he never knew him. Then there are the horrible memories when they watched him from a distance as he carried his cross and later hung on it while they squirmed in shame and self-disgust at their having forsaken him. Memories, finally, are present of more recent days which are filled with their wonder at his mysterious comings and goings. With all this preoccupation is there any wonder why their attention did not center on catching fish?

And now they hear his voice again: "Come and eat your meal." All the memories dissolve into reality; they are together again, and that is all that matters. There is the grill over the glowing embers, the fish on the grill, and the bread alongside. "Bring some of the fish you just caught," he tells them, and Peter hauls in the miraculous catch. Then they eat in silence, and not one of them presumes to inquire, "Who are you?" They know it is the Lord.

Now comes the real drama. You can feel the tenseness as Jesus turns to the man he had chosen as leader of his Church, the man who had three times denied having known him. He does not ask Peter if he is sorry, just, "Simon, son of John, do you love me?" Peter must be thinking: "This is a question I ought to be asking him." He does not answer: "Yes, I love you." He may not be all that sure of himself now. He says: "You know that I love you." Three times he has to answer Jesus' question, and finally with deepest anguish he adds, "Lord, you know everything. You know well that I love you."

We have here shades of the incident at Caesarea Philippi when Jesus asked Peter: "Who do people say that the Son of Man is? . . . Who do you say that I am?" Peter answers: "You are the Messiah, . . . the Son of the living God!" Jesus responds: "Blest are you, Simon son of Jonah! . . . you are 'Rock,' and on this rock I will build my church, and the jaws of death shall not prevail against it" (Matt 16:13-18).

Peter's answer to Jesus' question at Caesarea Philippi was the answer of his *head*, his *mind*. Now when Jesus asks "Do you love me?", Peter's answer, "Lord, you know everything. You know well that I love you," is the answer of his *heart*, or more exactly, of his mind *and* his heart. Now all of Peter—mind, heart, and will—is committed. Now and only now is he ready to assume his primacy, and today's Reading I shows how he exercises it.

But we must not assume that we have no part in this scene. Christ's question: "Who do you say that I am?" is also addressed to us, and we have to answer. It may be that the answer will first come from our minds. But inevitably the second question comes: "Do you love me?" Hopefully we are ready to reply: "Lord, you know everything. You know well that I love you." This is the answer of our heart, the only one Jesus wants to hear, the only one that will enable us to obey him when he calls out to us: "Come, follow me."

Lovely as this scene is, it is good to complete it with the vision of Jesus in heavenly glory as glimpsed by John in a vision:

> Worthy is the Lamb that was slain
> to receive power and riches, wisdom and strength,
> honor and glory and praise! . . .
> To the One seated on the throne,
> and to the Lamb,
> be praise and honor, glory and might,
> forever and ever!

If we ever felt like crying out "AMEN!", it is now. But we can say it with enthusiasm only because we have been privileged to be present at the homey cookout on the shores of that lake, seeing Jesus serving and hearing him ask: "Do you love me?"

273 MONDAY OF THE THIRD WEEK OF EASTER

READING I Acts 6:8-15
GOSPEL John 6:22-29

Reading I: The deacon Stephen, working great signs and wonders among the people, arouses the antagonism of the Synagogue of Roman Freedmen.

Gospel: Jesus continues his catechesis on the Eucharist.

Echoes of Easter continue to provide background for us as we enter the third week of the season.

> The Good Shepherd is risen! He who laid down his life for his sheep, who died for his flock, he is risen, alleluia (Entrance Antiphon).

He who laid down his life because he loved and cared for his flock could not be confined by death. But what matters most is how he continues to be our Shepherd now.

The deacon Stephen played an essential role in the early history of the Church. His complete self-dedication to Jesus, his willingness to die for him, make Stephen a model for all future martyrs, as well as for Christians of all time. Today he is on trial; tomorrow we shall see his sentence carried out. "Happy are they whose way is blameless" (Responsorial Psalm).

Jesus' teaching in today's gospel is most important for our understanding of the nature of the Eucharist and how he wants us to approach it. The crowd that had been fed by the miraculously multiplied loaves and fishes is on his trail. To be on the trail of Jesus to find him is a most praiseworthy design, but only if the seekers' desire and intention are pure. Jesus questions theirs:

> I assure you,
> you are not looking for me because
> you have seen signs
> but because you have eaten your fill
> of the loaves.

Their problem is that they do not see beyond food for the body; they do not understand Christ's will to nourish, not bodily physiques but *human persons* with "food that remains unto life eternal, food which the Son of Man will give you."

They do not understand, so, as often happens in such situations, they ask a question that does not seem to fit into the context of the discussion: "What must we do to perform the works of God?" It is the oldest question and the most modern: what do I have to *do*—what good work must I perform for God in order to win God's favor and possibly put him in debt to me? What a letdown his response must have been for them!

> This is the work of God:
> have faith in the One whom he sent.

In other words, you do not have to do anything; just let God do something for you.

What does having faith in Jesus mean? It means trust and confidence. It means saying yes to God. Above all it means an eager willingness to receive Jesus and all that he implies by way of truth, good news, divine concern, and caring *for you*. It means being willing to allow God to love you, even though you know you are not all that deserving of being so loved.

I have said that what matters most is how Jesus continues to be our Good Shepherd now. He does this by his deathless word, his teaching on what he has in mind for the real need of our lives, namely, the Eucharist. It is the greatest of the sacraments, for which he prepared the apostles and us with so much care and detail. And more is yet to come. Today's Opening Prayer is most appropriate:

> God our Father,
> your light of truth
> guides us to the way of Christ.
> May all who follow him
> reject what is contrary to the gospel.

We may wonder what is most contrary to the Gospel. It is refusal to remember how completely dependent on God our Creator we are, which is really what sin is. But may not the greatest obstacle to the effectiveness of the Gospel in our daily lives be this very concern for what we might accomplish for God by our own efforts? If we can put God in debt to us by our deeds, what need is there for a Savior, for a shepherd who lays down his life for his sheep?

To all who so want to do things for God (but really for themselves), Jesus says:

> Peace I leave with you, my own peace I give you; not as the world gives, do I give, alleluia (Communion Antiphon).

We respond: "Lord, . . . Strengthen us by this Easter sacrament" (Prayer after Communion) to show our willingness to accept the peace, the love, and the caring of Jesus, our Good Shepherd!

274 TUESDAY OF THE THIRD WEEK OF EASTER

READING I Acts 7:51-59
GOSPEL John 6:30-35

Reading I: Stephen condemns his persecutors and is in turn condemned and executed by them. Stephen dies, forgiving his executioners.

Gospel: Jesus says it is the Father who gives people "heavenly bread" and then claims to be that bread himself.

> Father,
> you open the kingdom of heaven
> to those born again by water and the Spirit.
> Increase your gift of love in us (Opening Prayer).

The liturgy continues to concern itself with the Church's newborn children, in fact, with all her members, no matter when they were baptized. What the Church wants most of all for them is *divine* love, the very love that exists in the Trinity. God knows that no one ever has enough of that kind of love. The human heart is limitless, both in capacity and desire. We want more, more, always more.

The prayer reminds us that divine love is a gift, and it cannot be self-generated or earned. What we can do is to respond to what Jesus did for us by dying and rising for us, and we can surely open our hearts wide to the outpouring of love that is always available, especially through the Eucharist.

No one phrases the ideal human attitude towards God more perfectly than the inspired psalmist who puts these words into our hearts today:

> In you, O Lord, I take refuge . . .
> my trust is in the Lord.
> I will rejoice and be glad of your kindness (Responsorial Psalm).

This prayer sums up the attitude of Jesus, of Mary, and of today's hero, Stephen. It is the only genuine attitude of the sincere follower of Christ. And surely Stephen's plea for forgiveness for his executioners—again in imitation of Jesus—is essential to the love we pray for today.

The Father's most effective answer to our prayer is the Eucharist, and today's gospel brings Jesus' instruction on its nature closer and closer to its climax. Jesus says:

> It is my Father who gives you the
> real heavenly bread.
> God's bread comes down from heaven
> and gives life to the world.

So there we have it again: everything that is good is from God, and it is freely given. In yesterday's gospel the people wanted to know what work they must do in order to perform the works of God. Now they want to know what work Jesus does that will make him worthy of being believed, and he tells them:

> It is my Father who gives you
> the real heavenly bread.

There is a hint that Jesus' hearers are arriving at a kind of understanding of his thinking. They realize that he is talking about a kind of nourishment that far surpasses in value the bodily food they have in mind: "Sir, give us this bread always."

Then come the unforgettable words:

> I myself am the bread of life.
> No one who comes to me shall ever be hungry,
> no one who believes in me shall thirst.

We who have heard these words so often, we who are so accustomed to the Eucharist, can hardly perceive how Jesus' teaching must have sounded in the ears of those who first heard him give it voice, and today's teaching is only the beginning. Coming gospels this week will be even more puzzling, not only to those first hearers, but also to us after all these years. Jesus calls himself "the bread of life," and he claims that those who eat this bread will never again be hungry.

In other words he is claiming that he and he alone is the answer to all human hungers and thirsts:

> No one who comes to me shall ever be hungry,
> no one who believes in me shall thirst.

Who can count the number of persons who have come to Jesus, who have believed in him and eaten the bread he promised—and have had the desires of their hearts fulfilled—since that day?

But it may be that even now we are still full of holy desire, and so we pray:

> Lord, . . .
> May the great joy you give us
> come to perfection in heaven (Prayer over the Gifts).

The human heart is limitless, both in capacity and desire. We want more, more, more—even of the greatest of all gifts, because it is the greatest of all God's gifts!

275 WEDNESDAY OF THE THIRD WEEK OF EASTER

READING I Acts 8:1-8
GOSPEL John 6:35-40

Reading I: The martyrdom of Stephen unleashes a new persecution of Christians in Jerusalem, but the apostles continue to preach and work miracles.

Gospel: Jesus continues his instruction on the Eucharist, with special emphasis today on the need for faith.

> Shout joyfully to God, all you on earth,
> sing praise to the glory of his name (Responsorial Psalm).

This joyous invitation or command to rejoice in the Lord belongs to the early Church in the flourishing of Christianity after Stephen's death. Stephen is with God, but the faith lives on. Jesus will not be denied. The signs and wonders he worked himself during his life on earth he continues now through his Church.

> Come and see the works of God,
> his tremendous deeds among men (Responsorial Psalm).

The praise and joy of the early Christians is now ours. "Fill me with your praise and I will sing your glory" (Entrance Antiphon). We celebrate the resurrection of Jesus now. It has been made present in our midst.

> Merciful Lord,
> hear the prayers of your people.
> May we who have received your gift of faith
> share for ever in the new life of Christ (Opening Prayer).

Today's gospel continues to teach how the Eucharist is to work, what it means, and what is necessary in the recipient of the sacrament if it is to be effective. "No one who comes to me shall ever be hungry, no one who believes in me shall ever thirst," says Jesus. But the people have difficulty believing him and believing in him, so he complains gently: "though you have seen me, you still do not believe."

Not only have they seen him, they have seen the wondrous deeds he has done, the *signs* like walking on water, multiplying loaves and fishes, healing the sick, and raising the dead.

But Jesus gives up on no one. He reassures the hesitant:

> All that the Father gives me shall
> come to me;
> no one who comes will I ever reject.

Then comes that mysterious phrase that does not quite seem to follow from what went before:

> because it is not to do my own will
> that I have come down from heaven,
> but to do the will of him who sent me.

This phrase describes Christ's whole philosophy of life, the motivation of all that he is and does: trusting obedience unto death. Now he seems to be giving an insight into the full nature of the obedience to which he is vowed:

> It is the will of him who sent me
> *that I should lose nothing of* what
> he has given me;
> rather, that I should raise it up on
> the last day (italics mine).

So it is the Father's will that Jesus should save and nourish us, but if, as his disciples, we would obey that divine will ourselves, it behooves us to allow Jesus to find us, allow him to love us. In a word we must *believe in him*, trust in him absolutely, and so have eternal life. Jesus says:

> Indeed, this is the will of my Father,
> that everyone who looks upon the Son
> and believes in him
> shall have eternal life.
> Him I will raise up on the last day.

If we are dissatisfied with the apparently few benefits we often seem to receive from the Eucharist, it might be well for us to look into the ideal Jesus lays down for us today. Do we see him in the signs he has worked as recorded in the gospels? Do we give our whole life over to him, doing the will of the Father as he consciously did, day in and day out?

We may never forget that the Eucharist for us is an *act of faith*. It demands faith. We may never take our faith for granted. The moment we do, we are in greatest danger of losing it. Faith needs constant, conscious refreshing, and that is the chief benefit of these post-Easter gospels and Masses for us.

Christ has risen and shines upon us, whom he has redeemed by his blood, alleluia (Communion Antiphon).

Lord, grant that I may see!

276 THURSDAY OF THE THIRD WEEK OF EASTER

READING I Acts 8:26-40
GOSPEL John 6:44-51

Reading I: God sends Philip to baptize the Ethiopian eunuch in whom he has planted the seed of faith.

Gospel: In his ongoing instruction on the Eucharist, Jesus emphasizes the need for faith: "he who believes has eternal life."

Whatever aspect of religion you consider, you always come back to the basic truth that it is the Lord who is our all. He gives everything, and he gives it gratis with no strings attached. You cannot earn or deserve God's self-giving, nor can you pay him once you have received. You can, of course, be grateful, but even your gratitude benefits you, rather than God. It makes you grow in grace and so opens you up to even greater desire for the fulfillment of all desire, God himself.

The Lord is my strength, and I praise him: he is the Savior of my life, alleluia (Entrance Antiphon).

This truth is marvellously dramatized in the story of the Ethiopian eunuch. It is obviously the Lord who has planted the thirst for the divine in the heart of this man and prompted him to seek the satisfaction for that thirst in the prophet Isaiah, even directing him to the passage:

Like a sheep he was led to the slaughter,
like a lamb before its sheerer he was silent.

It is the Spirit who sends Philip to the eunuch to bring his budding faith and his hunger for God to its flowering. Philip baptizes him and "the man went on his way rejoicing." Today's Responsorial Psalm expresses his emotions:

Shout joyfully to God, all you on earth,
Bless our God, you peoples,

> loudly sound his praise;
> He has given life to our souls.

In the gospel Jesus teaches the same truth:

> No one can come to me
> unless the Father who sent me draws him . . .
> "They shall all be taught by God,"
> Everyone who has heard the Father
> and learned from him
> comes to me.

Grace means gift. Faith means accepting the gift and opening the veins of our whole being to its blessed warmth, healing, and nourishing.

You may ask: how can I know if the Father is drawing me? And the answer is: you cannot *know*. When you know, you no longer believe. But the very fact that you read or listen attentively to the Gospel (like the Ethiopian reading Isaiah) is a reassuring sign that the Lord is drawing you.

The Eucharist, as Jesus explains it to us in John 6, is the most dramatic illustration of God-as-gift, God as self-giving.

> God so loved the world
> that he gave his only Son,
> that whoever believes in him may not die
> but may have eternal life (John 3:16).

Jesus so loves us that he gives himself to us in the Eucharist:

> I am the bread of life. . . .
> I myself am the living bread
> come down from heaven.
> If anyone eats this bread
> he shall live forever;
> the bread I will give
> is my flesh, for the life of the world.

At that dramatic point today's reading leaves off. Jesus is heading for a showdown with his hearers. Hopefully it will not be a showdown for us, but rather will make us want to "sing to the Lord, he has covered himself in glory" (Entrance Antiphon).

> Lord God,
> by this holy exchange of gifts
> you share with us your divine life.
> Grant that everything we do
> may be directed by the knowledge of your truth (Prayer over the Gifts).

One can wonder at the nature of that "holy exchange of gifts." The Lord certainly seems to be shortchanged. He gives us Jesus, the bread of life, and all we have to offer in return is a grateful heart.

But maybe that is all he wants, for a grateful heart is the best possible soil for an even greater outpouring of love, and pouring out love is what he seems to enjoy most. That is precisely what he has been trying to tell us since our own baptism and above all during the Lent and Holy Week just passed.

> Merciful Father,
> may these mysteries give us new purpose
> and bring us to a new life in you (Prayer after Communion).

277 FRIDAY OF THE THIRD WEEK OF EASTER

READING I Acts 9:1-20
GOSPEL John 6:52-59

Reading I: The persecutor Saul encounters Jesus on the Damascus road and is forever after a changed man, destined to become a very great apostle.

Gospel: Jesus' hearers do not understand how he can give his flesh to eat. He does not explain how. He simply demands faith.

> The Lamb who was slain is worthy to receive strength and divinity, wisdom and power and honor, alleluia.

This Entrance Antiphon takes us back again to Good Friday and reminds us of how it all began. And we leave today's Mass with another unforgettable reminder:

> The man who died on the cross has risen from the dead, and has won back our lives from death, alleluia (Communion Antiphon).

Jesus is the one who matters. What comes through to us from today's liturgy is that he never ceases the saving activity that he began when he preached in Israel. Reading I dramatically shows that though he has finished his saving work in the flesh he remains an interested and involved observer of how his Church is carrying on that work.

Saul has been the main opposition, so now it is time to take care of him, and Jesus does it in a rather sensational way. At one moment Saul is astride his horse, "breathing murderous threats against the Lord's disciples," the next he is lying on the ground, hearing a voice coming from he knows not where: "Saul, Saul, why do you persecute me?" "Who are you, sir?" Saul asks. The voice answers: "I am Jesus, the one you are persecuting."

The events that follow prepare Saul (and us) for his new career: his blindness, Ananias' laying on of hands, recovering his sight, his baptism, and the beginning of his preaching. Christ's words to Ananias indicate how he intends to use Saul as his apostle: "This man is the instrument I have chosen to bring my name to the Gentiles . . . and to the people of Israel. I myself shall indicate to him how much he will have to suffer for my name." How fitting the psalmist's response to that announcement:

> Go into the whole world and proclaim the good news.
> Praise the Lord, all you nations,
> glorify him, all you peoples!

"I am Jesus, the one you are persecuting." So Jesus identifies himself with the Christians Saul is persecuting. Paul never forgot those words. The revelation changed Saul's whole perception of life and people. He does not understand how Jesus and Christians can be one, how there can be identity between them, any more than he might try to understand how Jesus can change bread and wine into his Body and Blood for the nourishment of a starving world. He will meditate on this truth the rest of his life; it will be the foundation of his teaching and apostolate. So:

> The body of Christ is the body born of the Virgin Mary.
> The body of Christ is the body he offered on the altar of the cross.
> The body of Christ is the flesh he promises as food, which if anyone eats, he will live forever.
> The body of Christ is the Church in which he continues to live, preach, and heal through all ages.
> The body of Christ, the Church, makes present for all peoples what he did during his lifetime on earth.

"You, then, are the body of Christ. Every one of you is a member of it," this same Saul, now Paul, will one day write to the Corinthians and to us. "If one member suffers, all the members suffer with it; if one member is honored, all the members share its joy" (1 Cor 12:26-27).

"The Jews quarreled among themselves, saying: 'How can he give us his flesh to eat?'" states today's gospel. We who live now and who participate in this Mass and so many others two thousand years after Jesus first spoke the words of today's gospel cannot possibly grasp how mysterious—even horrifying—his words must have sounded to his first hearers. If those words seem like an invitation to sheer cannibalism, who can blame them for not believing him? We know it is not that, but that is about all we know. We will come back to this tomorrow, but meanwhile we will pray:

Lord,
may this eucharist,
which we have celebrated in memory of your Son,
help us to grow in love (Prayer after Communion).

278 SATURDAY OF THE THIRD WEEK OF EASTER

READING I Acts 9:31-42
GOSPEL John 6:60-69

Reading I: Peter prays over a dead woman and she is restored to life. Because of this miracle many come to believe in Jesus.

Gospel: Ending his discourse on the Eucharist, Jesus, still demanding faith, hints at a way his words may be understood.

As the texts of Friday's Mass brought back memories of Jesus' death, so today's remind us of his resurrection and our entering into his death and resurrection through baptism:

> In baptism we have died with Christ, and we have risen to new life in him, because we believed in the power of God who raised him from the dead, alleluia (Entrance Antiphon).

In Reading I we see Peter restoring the dead widow to new life: "Tabitha, stand up." She opens her eyes, looks at Peter, and sits up. After seeing the healing of a paralytic and other miracles, all signs worked in the name of Jesus, many people in the Lydda and Joppa areas receive the gift of faith. What Peter does for Tabitha, Jesus does for all who are baptized. We are dead, without divine life. Now it is ours. We have heard Paul's teaching in the Entrance Antiphon; he is even more explicit in Romans: "Through baptism into his death we were buried with him, so that, just as Christ was raised from the dead by the glory of the Father, we too might live a new life" (Rom 6:4-5).

Today's Mass is a miniature Easter Vigil, reminding us of what Jesus did for us when we were baptized. Our problem now and henceforward is to "not succumb to the influence of evil but remain true to your gift of life" (Opening Prayer).

In the gospel we hear some of the disciples responding to his discourse on the bread of life: "This sort of talk is hard to endure! How can anyone take it seriously?" Christ's reaction to their doubt must have been even more mysterious to them than it is to us now:

> Does it shake your faith? . . .
> What, then, if you were to see the Son of Man
> ascend to where he was before . . . ?
> It is the spirit that gives life;
> the flesh is useless.
> The words I spoke to you
> are spirit and life.

Jesus surely did not intend his flesh to be eaten in a cannibalistic sense, as some of his hearers undoubtedly thought. Some theologians think he is referring here to the sacramental reality of his presence, and I can settle for that. We believe that in the sacraments Jesus acts as really and truly as he did in his bodily presence. According to Fr. Bruce Vawter, when Jesus uses the words, flesh and blood, he is referring to his whole person. "Through the Eucharist the Christian is made to share in the life of Christ" (Bruce Vawter, *The Four Gospels* New York: Doubleday, 1967, 180).

The promise of Jesus is fulfilled at the Last Supper and at every Mass: "The Lord Jesus on the night in which he was betrayed took bread, and after he had given thanks, broke it and said, 'This is my body, which is for you. Do this in remembrance of me.' In the same way, after the supper, he took the cup, saying, 'This cup is the new covenant in my blood. Do this, whenever you drink it, in remembrance of me" (1 Cor 11:23-25).

The main point here is Jesus telling us that bread and wine become his Body and Blood. He does not tell us *how*. Throughout the discourse he has been demanding faith. He still demands it. We make Peter's words our own: "Lord, . . . You have the words of eternal life. We have come to believe; we are convinced that you are God's holy one" (Gospel).

> Lord,
> watch over those you have saved in Christ.
> May we who are redeemed by his suffering and death
> always rejoice in his resurrection (Prayer after Communion).

And may we always be sufficiently grateful for Jesus and his greatest of gifts to us, himself in the Eucharist.

> How shall I make a return to the Lord
> for all the good he has done for me?
> The cup of salvation I will take up,
> and I will call upon the name of the Lord . . .
> O Lord, . . . I am your servant, the son of your handmaid; . . .
> To you will I offer sacrifice of thanksgiving,
> and I will call upon the name of the Lord (Responsorial Psalm).

The psalmist better than anyone else tells us how to respond, not only to Jesus' discourse on the Eucharist but to every holy Mass.

FOURTH SUNDAY OF EASTER — Cycle A

READING I Acts 2:14, 36-41   READING II 1 Pet 2:20-25
GOSPEL   John 10:1-10

Reading I: This relates the results of Peter's first sermon on Pentecost: many are converted and ask Peter what they must do.

Reading II: The author of 1 Peter tells us that we must follow in Christ's footsteps and live in accord with God's will.

Gospel: Jesus compares himself to the gate of the sheepfold; whoever enters through him will be safe.

Reading I continues Peter's sermon on that first Christian Pentecost and gives the results. We are not told if these people were the same as those who used to hear Jesus condemn them for their blindness in refusing to accept him. But Peter does accuse them of having crucified Christ. If they were the same, we may wonder how it is that Peter's message converted them, whereas Jesus never had much success with them. It could well be that the grace resulting from the Savior's death and resurrection reached their hearts and made them ready for the power and enthusiasm of the Holy Spirit that filled Peter and the apostles that day and made his sermons so convincing.

The Responsorial Psalm, "The Lord is my shepherd; I shall not want," so dear to most Christians, is more a response to the gospel than to Reading I. It actually spells out the many meanings in the gospel. It tells of all our needs and how the Good Shepherd Jesus satisfies them: restful waters, food, guidance, comfort in sorrow, and freedom from fear of the present and the future—"The Lord is my shepherd; I shall not want."

Jesus takes care of all these needs (and any others that trouble us) for no other reason than that he is our shepherd and he knows each of us by name and loves us, one and all. Best of all he prepares a table for us, and, as Father Paschal Botz, O.S.B., puts it, he is the Shepherd, the Host, and the Food at God's table (*Runways to God*, The Liturgical Press, 47). We must not forget that this psalm is from the Old Testament, the Hebrew Bible, and it was written by Israel's greatest king and psalmist, David. His vision of the Lord God was truly prophetic!

Much of the pain, sorrow, and worry of daily life for anyone of any age could be calmed by a daily, trusting praying of this psalm.

The gospel is not the one most of us are familiar with. The one today is a kind of introduction to that one (which follows in this same chapter 10 of John). Today's reading speaks about the sheepfold and the ways it can be entered. The keeper of the sheepfold recognizes the true shepherd and lets him in. The marauder or thief knows he will not be recognized, so he climbs over the fence and tries to lead the sheep out. (It helps to understand this parable if we recall that Jesus is arguing with his enemies whom he accuses of being false shepherds, who exploit the people for their own profit.)

The true shepherd enters the sheepfold after being recognized by the gatekeeper and calls his sheep by name; they recognize his voice, follow him, and he leads them out to the green pastures. Then Jesus makes his claim:

> I am the gate.
> Whoever enters through me
> will be safe.
> He will go in and out,
> and find pasture.

Then he comes right out and tells us he is speaking not about dumb animals but about human persons, about us:

> I came
> that they might have life
> and have it to the full.

Not in today's gospel but following it in verse 11, Jesus says:

> I am the good shepherd;
> the good shepherd lays down his life
> for the sheep.

Perhaps now we are ready to grasp what the author of Reading II is telling us today: "Christ suffered for you . . . and left you an example, to have you follow in his footsteps. . . . In his own body he brought your sins to the cross, so that all of us, dead to sin, could live in accord with God's will. By his wounds you were healed." Then we return to the imagery of sheep and shepherd: "At one time you were straying like sheep, but now you have returned to the Shepherd, the Guardian of your souls."

There can be only one human response to this all-out manifestation of divine love and that is to pour out hearts in grateful love for our good shepherd, for those who are still straying and for those sheep who are overwhelmed by human misery of all kinds.

> I know my sheep
> and my sheep know me (John 10:14).

The only true test of knowing Christ is to follow in his footsteps and carry on his shepherding.

51   FOURTH SUNDAY OF EASTER   Cycle B

READING I   Acts 4:8-12   READING II   1 John 3:1-2
GOSPEL   John 10:11-18

Reading I: Peter, "filled with the Holy Spirit," tells the Elders that his healing of the cripple was done in the name of the Jesus they killed.

Reading II: John tells his Christians (and us) that we are God's children now, alive with the same divine life that is in the Father.

Gospel: Jesus tells his enemies and us that he is the good shepherd who knows his flock, who loves each one, and is willing to die for each.

> See what love the Father has bestowed on us
> in letting us be called children of God!
> Yet that is what we are (Reading II).

You almost have to catch your breath when the impact of those words sinks into your mind and heart. He is talking about you and me! I am a child of God? Yes, that is revealed truth. The same divine life that is in the three Persons of the Trinity is in us, it is our life too. "See what love the Father has bestowed on us!" This divine relationship is part of our celebration today.

Of course we are still celebrating the resurrection of Jesus, that crucial event that makes our relationship with the Father possible. The Alternate Opening Prayer spells out the practical consequences for daily living that result from what Jesus has done for us and what he is to us now:

> God and Father of our Lord Jesus Christ,
> though your people walk in the valley of darkness,
> no evil should they fear;
> for they follow in faith the call of the shepherd
> whom you have sent for their hope and strength.
> Attune our minds to the sound of his voice,
> lead our steps in the path he has shown,
> that we may know the strength of his outstretched arm
> and enjoy the light of your presence for ever.

In understanding the imagery of this gospel of the Good Shepherd, it is important not to see it in isolation but rather as part of the ongoing conflict between Jesus and his enemies among the Pharisaic leaders and in the context of his claim to be the Son of the Father and the light of the world. He follows the prophet Ezechiel (Chapter 34) in accusing these men of using their position of shepherding their people in order to benefit their own selfish interests instead of caring for their people, so God will take away their shepherding and become the shepherd himself. John sees all this coming true in Jesus (see Neal Flanagan, O.S.M., *Collegeville Bible Commentary: New Testament Series*, vol. 4, p. 50).

It is in this context that Jesus makes his claim today:

> I am the good shepherd;
> the good shepherd lays down his life
> for the sheep.
> The hired hand—who is no shepherd
> nor owner of the sheep—
> catches sight of the wolf coming
> and runs away, leaving the sheep
> to be snatched and scattered by the wolf.
> That is because he works for pay;
> he has no concern for the sheep.

We can imagine how Christ's enemies felt about such a portrayal of them and their attitudes. Shepherding of any kind is impossible without love and caring—loving concern for the entire flock and for each individual member.

Now in hearing and meditating on Christ's words, we hopefully see meanings in them that escaped the Pharisees. We know the extent of Christ's love for us from what happened to him after he first spoke the prophetic words of this gospel. His enemies crucified him, and he freely submitted to his own execution *out of love for us* and the desire to do his Father's will. But he rose from the dead so that he could continue to be our shepherd. The Communion Antiphon sums up his work perfectly:

> The Good Shepherd is risen! He who laid down his life for his sheep, who died for his flock, he is risen, alleluia.

There are few of our Lord's parables that are more important for our growth in intimacy with Christ and the fulfillment of our purpose in life. The Palestinian shepherd knew each of his sheep individually in all their vulnerability, and they knew him. When he called, they recognized his voice and they followed him wherever he led them. He never drove them, he *led*. He literally shared their life.

We know, of course, that Jesus is speaking about us, and we may not enjoy being compared to sheep. But Jesus does not intend that! God created us free, and he expects us to grow in that freedom. He expects us to make free, deliberate, intelligent decisions and choices. We receive the sacrament of confirmation to enable us to become mature adults, responsible for growing in our faith and sharing it.

What Jesus intends in telling us this parable is that we hear his voice calling us by name, that we recognize it as the one who loves us and proved it, and that we deliberately choose to get up and follow after him with a corresponding love. It is in this freely chosen following that we discover our true identity, our liberty.

> Attune our minds to the sound of his voice,
> lead our steps in the path he has shown,
> that we may . . .
> enjoy the light of your presence for ever (Alternative Opening Prayer).

52 FOURTH SUNDAY OF EASTER Cycle C

READING I Acts 13:14, 43-52 **READING II** Rev 7:9, 14-17
GOSPEL John 10:27-30

Reading I: Paul and Barnabas run into opposition from the nonbelieving Jews, but the Gentiles respond to their word with delight.

Reading II: John sees a vision of heaven in which he beholds all those who have "washed their robes and made them white in the blood of the Lamb."

Gospel: This is the conclusion of the parable of the Good Shepherd. Jesus says: "My sheep hear my voice. I know them, and they follow me."

The Good Shepherd is risen! He who laid down his life for his sheep, who died for his flock, he is risen, alleluia (Communion Antiphon).

"He is risen": these are the key words. If Jesus is to fulfill his promise to be our Good Shepherd, it was necessary that he be risen from the dead. Today we continue to celebrate his having risen, we celebrate his being our Good Shepherd.

Today's Mass is filled with the warmth of Christ's love for us all. The image of the Good Shepherd is the most precious, the most expressive, and surely the oldest of Christian symbols. The early Christians did not have the modern image of the Sacred Heart to tell them of Christ's love. They had the Good Shepherd, and they knew that it told them of his love for them. Jesus took this oldest and best known of all images and claims it for himself.

Whatever the best of human shepherds was for his flock, Jesus is to his flock, but multiplied to an infinite degree. "I am the Good Shepherd" (John 10:14), he says.

> My sheep hear my voice.
> I know them,

and they follow me.
I give them eternal life,
and they shall never perish.

There are depths beyond depths of meaning in Jesus' words: I *know* them; I know my own and my own know me. Christ's way of knowing is unlike that of anyone else. His knowing is a knowing not only of mind but of heart. It is shot through with love and esteem. He knows us with the same love and esteem that he knows the Father.

Jesus is the Good Shepherd to each of us personally and to all of us as a flock. He never gives up on anybody. If one sheep strays from the flock into sinful ways, he, the Good Shepherd, goes after the stray and brings it back, and the whole flock rejoices. Actually what this parable is all about is Christ's *believing* in each of us, his *trusting* us. Believing in and trusting each of us are what his love for us is all about. What he is telling us in this parable is that he is incapable of loving a little, incapable of loving only partially. His love for you and for me is overflowing; it is lavish in its extent and its depth.

Our God is not a tyrant God who seeks to win our loving obedience by threats. He is not a tantalizing God who holds out possible gifts to us if we are good. God does not love us because we are good or because we are especially lovable, but because we are who we are. He knows that loving and trusting us is risky, because he made us free. That was his idea. But it is a risk that he is willing to take, knowing also that we can never mature as whole persons unless we assume the responsibility that comes with our freedom. He knows, too, that unless we are free to sin, to reject his love, we cannot truly love him in return. God's fidelity to us does not depend—thank God!—on our fidelity to him.

Jesus has laid down his life for us. He has led us to the green pastures and the clear springs of the Eucharist where he continues to refresh and nourish us. This parable summarizes all that he has done for us out of love. Actually the parable tells us all that we need to know about religion and religious practice. Religion is not what we do for God. Religion is what we allow God to do for us. Do I really believe that God loves me? If not, why not? Do I think that my sins prevent him from loving me? If I do, then I go against all scriptural evidence. God is very fond of me. No matter how badly I have acted, no matter what sins I have committed, I cannot stop him from loving me. I do not understand this. It goes against all my human experience. But this is what Jesus and his divine Word tell me. So why don't I stop trying to be worthy of God's love for me and just let him love me?

279 MONDAY OF THE FOURTH WEEK OF EASTER

READING I   Acts 11:1-18
GOSPEL   John 10:1-10 or 10:11-18

Reading I: In a vision God tells Peter that the Gentiles do not have to become Jews or observe the dietary laws in order to be Christian.

Gospel: Using the image of a Good Shepherd, Jesus tells us that he loves and cares for all and is the answer to the thirsts of the human heart.

> As the hind longs for the running waters,
> so my soul longs for you, O God.
> Athirst is my soul for God, the living God (Responsorial Psalm).

There is no more basic fact of life than this irrepressible, ever-demanding thirst of the human heart for some kind of gratification, some satiety. From earliest ages those who know the human heart claim that the only one who can provide this deep-seated gratification is the one who created that heart and gave it its thirst. So we have the ancient psalmist crying out: "Send forth your light and your fidelity; they shall lead me on" (Responsorial Psalm).

Every heart experiences this thirst, whether it knows it or not. Humans are seekers by their very nature.

> O God, you are my God whom I seek;
> for you my flesh pines and my soul thirsts (Ps 63:2).

It was this human thirst for God that Peter was forced to recognize in the Gentiles and that prompted the opening up of the infant Church to the Gentiles. The more basic truth was that God hungered for Gentile love as much as for that of the Jews.

So hunger is mutual. It belongs both to God and to humans. Without it we die, or more exactly, without its satisfaction we die. Jesus is the final expression of God's desire to seek out and give himself to people. In the parable of the Good Shepherd, he describes how he satisfies himself and how he is himself our satisfaction.

He calls to his sheep, and they respond to his voice. He leads them out of the sheepfold, walking before them, leading them to the green pastures of the Eucharist, where he will slake their thirst and satisfy their hunger.

He goes on to present himself as the gate, the way, by which human hearts can enter into fulfillment. False shepherds who do not know the human heart try to present other kinds of satisfaction and fulfillment, but with no lasting success.

> I am the gate.
> Whoever enters through me

> will be safe.
> He will go in and out,
> and find pasture.
> The thief comes only to steal and slaughter and destroy.

What he is telling us is that salvation, happiness, the slaking of our human hungers, any kind of meaning for life can only come through him. Jesus sums up his entire life and work in the unforgettable phrase:

> I came
> that they might have life
> and have it to the full.

But back to the Responsorial Psalm: "Athirst is my soul for God, the *living* God" (italics mine). Jesus cannot be the ultimate satisfaction for our deathless desires unless he lives now. He is our Good Shepherd only because he lives. He proves his love for us by laying down his life for us, his flock. But he proves it most of all *by taking up that life again.*

> Christ now raised from the dead will never die again; death no longer has power over him, alleluia (Entrance Antiphon).

Without the resurrection the human heart would be forever frustrated.

But thirst can be dulled by sin; it may be turned aside by false quests which give momentary satisfaction. So we pray:

> Father,
> through the obedience of Jesus,
> your servant and your Son,
> you raised a fallen world.
> Free us from sin
> and bring us to the joy *that lasts for ever* (Opening Prayer) (italics mine).

280 TUESDAY OF THE FOURTH WEEK OF EASTER

READING I Acts 11:19-26
GOSPEL John 10:22-30

Reading I: The evangelization of the Gentiles continues. At Antioch the followers of Jesus are called Christians for the first time.

Gospel: Concluding Chapter 10 of John, Jesus describes his followers as those who hear his voice and follow him.

> Let us shout out our joy and happiness, and give glory to God, the Lord of all, because he is our King, alleluia (Entrance Antiphon).

I doubt that many of us Christians are all that enthusiastic, now that Easter is gradually fading into the past. Easter was one of those great "peak" experiences that some spiritual writers like to exalt, but who can stay on the peak indefinitely? What is important for us in our day-to-day, week-to-week Christian existence is that the memory of what the peak celebrated remains strong in our minds and hearts.

> Christ had to suffer and to rise from the dead, and so enter into his glory, alleluia (Communion Antiphon).

We go the same way.

The first reading shows the Church breaking out of its initial Jewish mold and spreading into a Catholic or universal mold. We modern Christians—Gentiles all—can have no idea of the pain and struggle this must have been for our Jewish ancestors in the faith. The Christian Church came out of Israel. Its roots, its first adherents, its Messiah-founder were all Jewish. So a bit of exclusive thinking on the part of the first Christians was understandable, although, as we shall see, some of them carried it too far.

At Antioch the disciples first receive the name Christian with all its immense connotations. Some of these connotations are spelled out in the gospel by none other than Christ himself. We are still in the tenth chapter of John, and Jesus is winding up his discourse on the Good Shepherd. It is the Feast of the Dedication of the Temple, commemorating the rededication of the Temple by Judas Maccabeus in 165 B.C.E. It is winter, and Jesus is walking in the temple area.

Soon he is surrounded by a group of Jews who demand, "How long are you going to keep us in suspense? If you really are the Messiah, tell us so in plain words." He responds:

> The works I do in my Father's name
> give witness in my favor,
> but you refuse to believe.

Works, miraculous signs, are the most powerful and expressive kind of language, but if the hearers have closed up their minds and hearts,

67

no evidence will succeed in penetrating into their consciences. They see love in action, they hear him, they see others rejoicing in what he has done, but they do not choose to hear. They are unwilling to belong to his flock. It is a replay of original sin. God reveals himself as Light, Love, Truth, Mercy, and Goodness in Person, and many refuse to accept him. Such is the mystery of human freedom.

Jesus then comes to the perfect characterization of the Christian:

> My sheep hear my voice . . . .
> and they follow me.
> I give them eternal life,
> and they shall never perish.
> No one shall snatch them out of my hand.

It sounds so simple until you start analyzing all that is involved in hearing his voice, following him, and being willing to receive eternal life. To hear Jesus is to open your whole inner self to his Word and above all to his love. To follow him is to make him and his Gospel, his mind, his attitudes, your very own way of life. It is to center your life in him, to live for him, and if necessary to die for him. It is to allow him to love you without fear of his overdoing it.

> Almighty God,
> as we celebrate the resurrection,
> may we share with each other
> the joy the risen Christ has won for us (Opening Prayer).

We do not ask God to keep us on the Easter peak. What we need more than that is the courage and the willingness to hear the voice of Jesus, his Son, and above all the courage to follow him wherever he wishes to lead us. May the Lord help us to *be* what he has called us to be, Christians, not only in name, but in our inmost hearts!

281 WEDNESDAY OF THE FOURTH WEEK OF EASTER

READING I Acts 12:24–13:5
GOSPEL John 12:44-50

Reading I: We continue to hear about the dynamic progress of the early Church. The Holy Spirit is obviously in charge.

Gospel: Jesus reveals himself as the light of the world. He is the manifestation of the Father. To heed him is to heed the Father.

> The Lord says, I have chosen you from the world to go and bear fruit that will last, alleluia (Communion Antiphon).

These are Christ's words to his apostles, his words to the first Christian community, his words to us all. With their Hebrew background of awareness of being God's chosen people, the early Christians were especially partial to this truth, but now they saw in it deeper and more attractive meanings. They became apostolic, they were enthusiastic in their determination to spread their faith, and Reading I gives details.

What happened to those first Christians was that Christ entered into their lives through some channel—the preaching of one of the apostles or simply the evidence of the common life of the Christians—and they were forever transformed. They lost their hearts to Christ, and he in turn restored those hearts to them, inflamed now with the desire and determination to share with others.

> I will be a witness to you in the world, O Lord. I will spread the knowledge of your name among my brothers, alleluia (Entrance Antiphon).

True love is never possessive. To love as those early Christians loved meant wanting Jesus to be loved more and more by more and more. Love compelled; love drove them on. This fact emerges again and again in our readings from Acts and above all in the Letters of one of the world's greatest lovers, Paul the Apostle. The reason for that kind of spirit was that divine Love, the Holy Spirit, was in charge of operations. The presence and leadership of the Spirit is simply taken for granted in that community of Christ's chosen ones. Today we see the Holy Spirit determining who is to be sent out to spread the Word and where they are to go. Three times the Spirit is mentioned in the reading, and those selected are said to have been "sent forth by the Holy Spirit."

Yesterday's gospel ended with Christ's words, "The Father and I are one." Today he draws some important conclusions from that deep truth.

> Whoever puts faith in me
> believes not so much in me

> as in him who sent me;
> and whoever looks on me
> is seeing him who sent me.

What Jesus is saying is that he is a sacrament; he is the Sacrament, the manifestation of the Godhead in all its goodness, wisdom, power, light, and love for humankind. Jesus in turn manifests himself and all that he is in and through the Church in her sacraments.

May we not forget that we Christians are the Church. Each of us is or can be a sacrament through whom Christ wishes to communicate himself to our world, as he did through the apostolic community we read about in Reading I. Do we ever think of asking ourselves if non-Christians are reminded of Christ when they see us or hear us or observe our way of life and system of values? If we are not concerned about being "sacraments" to others, then maybe the light within us, namely Christ, has grown dim, and that is not good, either for us or for the world.

Two days ago we prayed, "My soul longs for you, O God" (Monday's Responsorial Psalm). Today we pray:

> Fill our emptiness
> with the blessing of this eucharist,
> the foretaste of eternal joy" (Opening Prayer).

Is God telling us that the Eucharist is the answer to our hearts' desire? I think I can settle for that, at least until the time comes when the vision of Jesus by way of sacramental sign gives way to the vision of that same Jesus face-to-face.

> May the peoples praise you, O God;
> may all the peoples praise you (Responsorial Psalm).

282 THURSDAY OF THE FOURTH WEEK OF EASTER

READING I Acts 13:13-25
GOSPEL John 13:16-20

Reading I: In the synagogue at Antioch, Paul gives his hearers a lesson in Hebrew history, all leading up to the coming of Jesus, the Son of God.

Gospel: At the Last Supper Jesus washes his disciples feet and claims to fulfill the prophecies by claiming to be God: I AM.

Today's Mass takes us back into the distant past, leads us into the meaning of the present, and opens a way to a future goal.

Perhaps the best place to start is with Paul in the synagogue at Antioch. The leader of the synagogue invites him to speak, and Paul responds with a lesson in history. He takes his hearers back to the sojourn of the Jews in Egypt, their rescue by God, their wandering in the desert, and their subsequent history through the periods of the Judges and Kings down to the coming of John the Baptist and Jesus.

> When you walked at the head of your people, O God, and lived with them on their journey, the earth shook at your presence (Entrance Antiphon).

This verse from Psalm 68 points to the deep-seated belief of the Jews that it was God himself who had chosen them and walked with them through their history after rescuing them from slavery. Their God is a God of love, whose favors they will sing for all eternity:

> through all generations my mouth
> shall proclaim your faithfulness (Responsorial Psalm).

The greatest proof of God's loving care for his people is in sending his Son Jesus as "a savior for Israel" (Reading I).

> Jesus Christ, you are the faithful witness, firstborn from the dead; you have loved us and washed away our sins in your blood (Gospel Verse).

The gospel shows us this Jesus at the Last Supper the night before his death. He has just given his disciples (and us) a vivid example of true loving service by washing their feet. Now he tells them that he is the fulfillment of all the prophecies and promises contained in the past history of their people as recorded in Scripture:

> My purpose here is the fulfillment of Scripture . . .
> I tell you this now . . .
> so that when it takes place you may believe
> that I AM.

That claim belongs only to God, the Lord most high. This was the name he himself chose in describing who he was to Moses. Since no human being dared to use this expression, Jesus here claims to be God, equal to the Father in all. He is one who walks at the head of his people now and lives with them on their pilgrimage to the promised land, and we are that people!

After his resurrection and just before his ascension, he will nail down his claim:

> I, the Lord, am with you always, until the end of the world (Communion Antiphon).

So the journey begun when God walked at the head of his people out of Egypt continues on now, and we are part of it. It is a saving journey for each of us and for our world. Since this is a journey of faith, we do not know the immediate future. Only the ultimate goal is assured. But we are not alone. We have no fear. He is with us always until the end.

> My faithfulness and my kindness
> shall be with him,
> and through my name shall his
> horn be exalted.
> "He shall say of me, 'You are my father,
> my God, the Rock, my savior'" (Responsorial Psalm).

So we ask the Father to keep us in his love and sustain us as we go on and on. There are times when we seem so alone and life seems so difficult. May he help us to remember all that he has done for his people through the ages. May he help us to believe in his never-dying love for us!

> Almighty and ever-living Lord,
> you restored us to life
> by raising Christ from death.
> Strengthen us by this Easter Sacrament;
> may we feel its saving power in our daily life (Prayer after Communion).

283 FRIDAY OF THE FOURTH WEEK OF EASTER

READING I Acts 13:26-33
GOSPEL   John 14:1-6

Reading I: Paul continues his sermon in the Antioch synagogue, reminding the Jews how Jesus fulfilled the Old Testament prophecies.

Gospel: Jesus comforts his troubled apostles; he assures them that he is the way, and the truth, and the life.

The Friday liturgy continues to be as special in the Easter season as it was during Lent. Apparently the Church believes that there is special value for us both to look forward to and back upon Good Friday, so today we look back:

> By your blood, O Lord, you have redeemed us from every tribe and tongue, from every nation and people: you have made us into the kingdom of God, alleluia (Entrance Antiphon).

Paul also refers to the crucifixion in the continuation of his sermon in the Antioch synagogue. As was his custom, he speaks to his fellow Jews against the background of their sacred history. They are "children of the family of Abraham." He also recalls the tragic execution of Jesus because the leaders of the Jerusalem community "failed to recognize him" for what he was, namely the fulfillment of Jewish prophecy. Then he comes to his dramatic conclusion: "We ourselves announce to you the good news that what God promised our fathers he has fulfilled for us, their children, in raising up Jesus, according to what is written in the second psalm, 'You are my son; this day I have begotten you.'"

Each word in that quote from the psalm is significant. It is the Father who salutes his Son: "You are my son; this day I have begotten you." We touch here at the heart of the Christian doctrine of the Trinity. In human speech habits and ways of thought, a father is naturally older than and superior to his son. The mystery of the Trinity insists that in the Trinity there is no such priority for the Father. Each person is coequal and coeternal. "This day" refers to the day of eternity, and eternity means that there is no beginning, no past, no future. With God it is always NOW. God the Father is from all eternity; the Son is from all eternity; the Holy Spirit is from all eternity.

God the Son became man through the power of the Holy Spirit and the consent of Mary. He who existed before all ages, who is God, second Person of the blessed Trinity, becomes man, grows as a human being, preaches, works miracles, founds a Church, suffers, dies, and is buried. But as Paul tells us today, God raised him up according to the Psalm: "You are my son, this day I have begotten you." As we have said, "this day" is the day of eternity. But may we not also conclude that "this day" is also the day of the resurrection, when Jesus the Son is reestablished into his rightful relationship of equality with the Father?

It is this Jesus who speaks to us today, telling us that he is our way, our truth, our life. The gospel, of course, takes us back to the Last Supper, to his last communication to the apostles before he died. His advice to them is still valid for us: "Do not let your hearts be troubled." Who of us does not have problems of varying degrees of seriousness? Jesus does not ask us to pretend the troubles are not there. He simply wants us to know that, since he is with us now in a very special way, we must try not to let the problems defeat us or make us bitter.

"Have faith in God and faith in me," he asks. In other words trust me, have confidence in me, for I am with you, in you, and you are in me. Together we can overcome. Jesus' words to the apostles at the Last Supper ought to support us more than they supported the apostles, because we know, as they did not, that

> Christ our Lord was put to death for our sins; and he rose again to make us worthy of life, alleluia (Communion Antiphon).

May we who are redeemed by his suffering and death always rejoice in his resurrection, *"for he is Lord for ever and ever"* (Prayer after Communion) (italics mine). May all troubled hearts give way to that consoling truth!

284 SATURDAY OF THE FOURTH WEEK OF EASTER

READING I Acts 13:44-52
GOSPEL John 14:7-14

Reading I: Paul and Barnabas run into opposition in the Antioch synagogue, as a result they delight the Gentiles by promising to come to them.

Gospel: Jesus claims oneness with the Father and assures the apostles that anything they ask in his name he will do.

Easter Season Saturdays, like its Fridays, bring back happy memories, either of our own baptisms or of their renewal four weeks ago tonight. We readily recall the marvellous symbols of that night: the new light, the Easter candle entering the darkened church to tell us that Jesus had risen from the dead, the blessing and sprinkling of the new baptismal water, the baptisms, and the renewal of baptism. Then there were the Old Testament readings pointing to the meaning of our new birth in baptism. Perhaps the most dramatic effect of all was the spread of the light of the Easter candle to the candles of every person in church, telling us we were one people, alive with new life from the risen Lord. And remember how with one voice and heart we reaffirmed our common faith in our triumphant head newly risen from the dead?

Today's Entrance Antiphon reminds us again of the deep meaning of it all:

> You are a people God claims as his own, to praise him who called you out of darkness into his marvelous light, alleluia.

That was four weeks ago. But the fervor, the enthusiasm, the excitement of that glorious night may have waned. Hence the urgency of today's Opening Prayer:

> Father,
> may we whom you renew in baptism
> bear witness to our faith by the way we live.
> By the suffering, death, and resurrection of your Son
> may we come to eternal joy.

In a word our baptism into the death and resurrection of Christ imposes responsibility, that of sharing it by living it. We are—or ought to be—all involved in carrying the redeeming work of Jesus to the end that eventually "All the ends of the earth [will see] the salvation by our God" (Responsorial Psalm). Christianity still has a long way to go, not only geographically but interiorly into our minds, our hearts, and our whole being.

There is not much point in celebrating Lent and Easter year after year unless we are willing to open our minds and hearts to the conversion of life the celebration implies and requires. "If you stay in my word, you will indeed be my disciples," Jesus tells us, as he told the apostles, "and you will know the truth" (Gospel Verse). Jesus needs disciples now just as much as he needed them then.

What Paul and Barnabas said to the Jews in the Antioch synagogue is true of each of us as Christians and of all of us together: "a people God claims as his own" (Entrance Antiphon). "I have made you a light to the nations, a means of salvation to the ends of the earth." This does not mean that we all have to go out to be missionaries, as Paul and Barnabas were or as so many modern missionaries still are. But it does mean, or ought to mean, a much deeper awareness of our *being members of a missionary Church* than we have had in the past. We still have a long way to go, mainly because too many Christians have failed to recognize that the Catholic faith the Lord has given them imposes the obligation of sharing it, not just taking comfort in it.

In the gospel Jesus takes us back to the Last Supper. The assurance Jesus gave to the apostles he now intends for us: "whatever you ask in my name I will do." Anything whatever, Lord? Then here is my prayer:

> Lord,
> may this eucharist . . .
> help us to grow in love (Prayer after Communion).

And may it be a love that never allows us to forget that we are members of an apostolic, missionary Church!

53 FIFTH SUNDAY OF EASTER   Cycle A

READING I Acts 6:1-7   **READING II** 1 Peter 2:4-9
GOSPEL John 14:1-12

Reading I: Because of the demands of preaching the good news, the apostles ordain seven men who will be their helpers in caring for the needs of the people.

Reading II: Writing to prospective converts, St. Peter describes the Church as a building made up of living stones, with Christ as cornerstone.

Gospel: At the Last Supper Jesus begs his apostles not to lose heart, but to trust in him, for he is the way, the truth, and the life.

Jesus speaks to us today, just as he did to the apostles at the Last Supper:

> I am indeed going to prepare a place for you,
> and then I shall come back to take you with me,
> that where I am you also may be. . . .
> I am the way, and the truth, and the life (Gospel).

Naturally we conclude that he is speaking about his ascension. But possibly there may be another interpretation, that Jesus is speaking about another kind of presence in which *he is with us now* and that we do not have to wait for another life in which to meet him and come to know and live with him, and he with us.

Because of human limitations we usually think of the events of Christ's life after the resurrection as successive, covering fifty days. But more and more spiritual writers are helping us understand that those last fifty days of his life on earth constituted one great event which has marvellous meaning for us now. The meaning is that Jesus entered into a new kind of existence, not somewhere in another world but here in this world, in this Church, his people, in redeemed humanity. And it is in this Church—in us—that he continues his words and saving works.

What a new and exciting insight this idea gives to Jesus' words today: "I am indeed going to prepare a place for you . . . *that where I am you also may be*" (italics mine). Above all there is that other exciting phrase: "I am the way, and the truth, and the life"—not "I *was*, or I *will be*, but *I am.*"

> I am the vine and you are the branches . . . he who lives in me, and I in him, will bear much fruit (Communion Antiphon).

There can be no doubt about Christ's desire to live with us and to have us live in and with him. Whether or not he actually is our way, our truth, and our life depends on our welcoming him into our minds and hearts without fear of the consequences. There is a difference between living and existing. We do not need Christ in order to *exist*, but we surely need him in order to *live*.

How are we to understand "I am the way, and the truth, and the life"? At least part of the answer to that question depends on what we are as Christians, and Peter in Reading II tells us that we are " 'a chosen race, a royal priesthood, a holy nation, a people he [God] claims for his own to proclaim the glorious works' of the One who called you from darkness into his marvelous light." Peter also tells us that we are "living stones, built as an edifice of spirit, into a royal priesthood, offering spiritual sacrifices acceptable to God through Jesus Christ."

So to live means sharing in Christ's priestly work and sharing in his redeeming life, including his passion, death, and resurrection. Living in Christ includes living to the fullest of our capacity as human beings, with eyes and minds and hearts open to joy, to beauty, and to truth. It means never to stop growing mentally and spiritually, never to give up learning, never to cease loving, and never to close our eyes to the wonderment of life.

He wants to be our way, our truth, our life, but we have to allow him to enter. This means sharing his vision of the entire world reconciled to the Father—if that does not seem too vague. It means having his sensitivity to the plight of the poor, the hungry, the aged, the ill. We are rightfully concerned, even horrified, at the tragedy of violence in our world, but so often we seem completely unconcerned about the further tragedy of so many who never learn to *live* once they have been born, about those who "retire" from life. We can retire from a job; we should never retire from life. Once we stop growing, learning, loving, reflecting, thanking, rejoicing, praising God, we die. Death is the absence of life; too many are dead long before they are embalmed.

How essential is our Prayer after Communion today:

> Merciful Father,
> may these mysteries give us new purpose
> and bring us to a *new life in you* (italics mine).

To live is to be human. To live is to grow, to change, and to develop our insights into the good news of Christ, the Word of God. To live is never to be satisfied with any present condition of life, with what we know, with whatever progress we have made in acquiring a skill or a profession. We can always improve, always live more deeply. To live is to be able to choose: to choose oneself, one's identity, to choose to live to the fullest of our capacity day by day. "He who *lives in me*, and *I in him*, will bear much fruit."

In the Prayer over the Gifts we ask God to share with us his divine life by means of "this holy exchange of gifts." We go on:

> Grant that everything we do
> may be directed by the knowledge of your truth.

What is the truth we may never lose sight of? Jesus has the answer:

> I am the way, and the truth, and the life;
> no one comes to the Father but through me   (Gospel).

54 FIFTH SUNDAY OF EASTER — Cycle B

READING I   Acts 9:26-31   READING II   1 John 3:18-24
GOSPEL   John 15:1-8

Reading I: This relates Saul's difficulties being accepted by the Christians. Saul persists and is even threatened with death.

Reading II: John tells us that we must believe in Jesus and love one another with all our being.

Gospel: Using the imagery of the vine and the branches, Jesus describes the intimacy of his relationship with us.

Today's Mass contains a variety of moods and emotions; the memory of Easter lingers on, of course, and it is not hard to obey the Church's recommendation to

> Sing to the Lord a new song, for he has done marvelous deeds; he has revealed to the nations his saving power (Entrance Antiphon).

And we can only hope that the Father will hear our prayer:

> you have revealed to the nations your saving power
> and filled all ages with the words of a new song.
> Hear the echo of this hymn.
> Give us voice to sing your praise
> throughout this season of joy (Alternative Opening Prayer).

The predominant mood of the Easter season continues to be one of joy at the victory of Jesus over death. The Responsorial Psalm carries on that mood with one of the most attractive verses in all the psalms: "May your hearts be ever merry!"

But the Christian life, even during this season of joy, is not all rejoicing. We have to live, we are still human, we still have problems. This life, however, does assume a very deep meaning when we see it in the light of the readings from John's First Letter and the fifteenth chapter of his gospel, and they belong together.

The apostles were plain men. We can imagine how puzzled they must have been at some of the language Jesus uses. They are at the Last Supper and Jesus says to them:

> I am the true vine
> and my Father is the vinegrower. . . .
> I am the vine, you are the branches.
> He who lives in me and I in him
> will produce abundantly.

Being compared to branches growing out of the vinestock was not the kind of language they were accustomed to.

We know now, of course, that Jesus was speaking with images, that he was trying to bring home to them their true relationship with him and with one another. We realize, too, that Jesus is now speaking to us, telling us that as the branch grows out of the trunk or vinestock and is alive with the very same life sap that is in the trunk, so are we all alive with his life, his love, his vitality.

He says to us today: "Live on in me, as I do in you." What this extraordinary statement does to our lives is to bring Jesus out of the past, out of history, and into the present, into the NOW of our existence. It can change the whole outlook of our life. It wipes out the distinction between the sacred and the secular in daily living, between the religious and the worldly. It makes all life sacred.

In other words we are not being religious only when we are at Mass or on our knees in prayer. We are being religious when we live, work, and suffer, when we play, study, even when we sleep. We are being religious because the Son of God is living in us and with us, and it is his life that we live as well as our own. All of life becomes prayer, because he is living and praying in us.

Jesus speaks of his Father as the vinegrower who prunes away barren branches and trims the fruitful ones. Traditionally this verse has been interpreted as referring to the suffering in our lives. It may be better for us to understand it in the context of Jesus' words:

> the fruitful ones [branches]
> he trims clean
> *to increase their yield* (italics mine).

This greater yield is a deeper intimacy with him, contributing to the overall holiness and effectiveness of the Church, the true vine and all its branches.

We may not overlook the additional truth that comes through from the image of the vine and the branches, namely our relationship with one another. A vine or tree and its branches form one. Many branches grow out of the same trunk; all the branches are alive with the life principle in the trunk. "Live on in me, as I do in you," says Jesus, and the "you" is in the plural. So we are back again with the familiar idea of love, charity, forgiveness towards one another, including members of all races and religions. The vine and the branches which is Christ grows universally, and it grows on love, the same love in us that is in him.

After many years of meditating on his beloved Master's words about the vine and the branches, the disciple John wrote:

> Little children,
> let us love in deed and in truth
> and not merely talk about it. . . .
> His commandment is this:

we are to believe in the name of his Son, Jesus Christ,
and are to love one another as he commanded us.
Those who keep his commandments remain in him
and he in them (Reading II).

The vine and the branches which is the Church is still a long way from having reached its full flowering and growth. Its beginnings in the life, death, and resurrection of Jesus could not have been better. How much do we realize that much of its future growth and flowering depends a great deal upon our becoming fruitful branches?

55   FIFTH SUNDAY OF EASTER   Cycle C

READING I Acts 14:21-27   **READING II** Rev 21:1-5
GOSPEL John 13:31-35

Reading I: We read and hear the account of Paul's first missionary journey, including Paul's "warning" to his converts that they would have to undergo many trials for their faith.

Reading II: We share John's vision of the end of time, when Jesus will come again and the universe and all peoples will be forever reconciled with the Creator.

Gospel: Judas has departed, and we receive Jesus' final command: "Love one another. Such as my love has been for you, so must your love be for each other."

Remembering and celebrating the past, the Church today also looks ahead into the distant future. Easter, of course, is still very much in our minds and our hearts, and we gladly heed the command:

> Sing to the Lord a new song, for he has done marvelous deeds; he has revealed to the nations his saving power (Entrance Antiphon)

in raising up our beloved Savior, Jesus Christ.

Reading I gives us details on how that revelation was carried out and shared with the nations. We can follow Paul and Barnabas along their apostolic travels through Asia Minor. The apostles, especially Paul, are *driven* men, that is, they are impelled by their love for Jesus. It would almost seem as though they cannot help themselves. Their love for him makes them want him to be loved by more and more people everywhere. The worst possible trials are to be expected by anyone who loves as they do, so Paul reassures and encourages his converts with the instruction: "We must undergo many trials if we are to enter into the reign of God."

> Let all your works give you thanks, O Lord,
> and let your faithful ones bless you.
> I will extol you, O my God and King,
> and I will bless your name forever and ever (Responsorial Psalm).

It is the gospel that tells us where Paul and Barnabas (and every other disciple, including ourselves) can derive the love and courage that drives them. Jesus is coming to the end of his discourse at the Last Supper. He says:

> My children, I am not to be with you much longer. . . .
> I give you a new commandment:
> Love one another.
> Such as my love has been for you,
> so must your love be for each other.

Would that we Christians were as careful about keeping *this* commandment of the Lord as we are about keeping the ones he gave us on Mount Sinai! Love for one another is *the* distinguishing mark of the follower of Christ. There is no other.

> This is how all will know you for my disciples:
> your love for one another.

Mutual love between Christians will also be the most convincing argument to non-Christians of the genuineness of the Gospel, the argument that will do more to attract and draw other persons to become Christians than a library full of arguments. Paul understood this and that is why he was so intent on forming communities of faith in Gentile lands, zealous groups who, by making mutual love their way of life, drew others to the faith. This kind of missionary endeavor is still valid and possible for every Christian parish and religious community, if we only realized it.

But everything that today's liturgy brings to mind—the death and resurrection of Jesus, the missionary work of the apostles and their successors through the centuries, the apostolic work of parishes and religious communities in the last twenty centuries, and all that still remains to be done—aims at accomplishing the vision of Christ's second coming described so graphically by John in Reading II. John sees the holy city, Jerusalem, coming down out of heaven, "beautiful as a bride prepared to meet her husband." And he hears a heavenly voice cry out: "This is God's dwelling among men. He shall dwell with them and they shall be his people and he shall be their God. . . . He shall wipe every tear from their eyes, and there shall be no more death or mourning, . . . for the former world has passed away."

The vision of that future may seem like a long way off. It appears quite certain that it will not come in our lifetime. The Lord is going to have to wipe away countless tears of pain and sorrow from our eyes before he calls us to our heavenly home where we can await the second coming with joyous anticipation.

However, there is an exciting and not too well-known truth of our faith that makes it possible for us to share in and celebrate the past and future deeds of Christ, his entire redeeming act, here and now, without having to wait in heaven for the actual happening. The "redeeming act" of Christ included not only his historical life, death, and resurrection but also his second coming at the end of time. And every time we celebrate the Mass, obeying his command, "Do this in memory of me," *that entire redeeming act is made present for us* here and now; it is a present reality. So we do not have to go back into the past or into the future by means of an imaginary trip, we celebrate that entire redeeming act here and now.

This is the incredible privilege of sharing in the Eucharist; this is the new song that fills all the ages (see Alternative Opening Prayer). "See, I make all things new!" (Reading II) says the One who sits on the throne. There can be only one response from us: I will praise your name forever, my King and my God.

285 MONDAY OF THE FIFTH WEEK OF EASTER

READING I Acts 14:5-18
GOSPEL John 14:21-26

Reading I: In Lystra Paul heals a crippled man and has to resist the people's wish to worship him as a god.

Gospel: Jesus promises the Holy Spirit who will remind the apostles of all that he has told them. He also reveals the indwelling of the three divine persons in all who love him.

We continue to remember and to celebrate the resurrection of Jesus:

> The Good Shepherd is risen! He who laid down his life for his sheep, who died for his flock, he is risen, alleluia (Entrance Antiphon).

He is with us now.

We are also present at a fascinating episode in the apostolic careers of Paul and Barnabas, who continue to preach the resurrection of Jesus along with his saving concern for the Gentiles. Paul heals a cripple in the name of the risen Christ, and as a result the crowd wants to worship them as gods. The horrified Paul does his best to correct their idolatrous impulses, even giving them a lesson in elementary theology.

Look at the world around you, Paul tells the people. It could not have just happened; it must have had a Creator-God who sends down rain and rich harvests upon the people and fills their spirits with food and delight. It is a familiar argument that Paul uses more than once, with varying degrees of success, in his attempts to convince the pagans of the existence of the one true God.

The Responsorial Psalm sums up the whole situation for Paul and Barnabas, and also provides us with a heart-warming lesson in theology:

> Not to us, O Lord, not to us
> but to your name give glory
> because of your kindness, because of your truth. . . .
> Our God is in heaven;
> whatever he wills, he does. . . .
> May you be blessed by the Lord,
> who made heaven and earth.

We may not miss the deep truth illustrated by the actions of these pagan peoples: the fact of the hunger of the human heart for God. Their hunger may be somewhat tainted by the desire for a wonder-working God who could heal all their ills, but they did want a God they could see and hear, talk to, and worship. Paul wants to give them Jesus as *the* answer to their hearts' desire, but tomorrow's reading will tell us of his failure.

Today another theme is added to our happy remembering of the resurrection, namely Jesus' promise of the Holy Spirit:

> the Paraclete, the Holy Spirit
> whom the Father will send in my name,
> will instruct you in everything,
> and remind you of all that I told you (Gospel).

The emphasis here is on the teaching and reminding function of the Holy Spirit. All the things Jesus taught while he was with them—far from being forgotten—will be brought back into their consciousness by the Spirit. And then, too, for the first time they will understand, not just with their reason but with their heart, what he was saying to them during those three blessed years of their training.

This promise of the Holy Spirit is now for and to us; it is a promise that will be fulfilled this year at Pentecost. Please God that the Spirit will at long last help us to grasp the full import of Jesus' promise:

> Anyone who loves me
> will be true to my word,
> and my Father will love him;
> we will come to him
> and make our dwelling place with him (Gospel).

What people from the beginning of human consciousness have longed for, what Paul's hearers unknowingly desired, is now ours. We, human persons that we are, are the dwelling place of the most high God! God wants to dwell in us, to be *at home* in our hearts, but he cannot be at home in us unless we welcome him with open hearts and great desire. He wants to be a welcome, beloved guest, not one who forces his way in.

In the Opening Prayer we beg God the Father to "help us to seek the values that will bring us eternal joy in this changing world." The greatest of all values is awareness of the transforming indwelling of the three persons of the Blessed Trinity in us. Come, Holy Spirit, INSTRUCT OUR HEARTS!

286 TUESDAY OF THE FIFTH WEEK OF EASTER

READING I Acts 14:19-28
GOSPEL John 14:27-31

Reading I: Despite persecution Paul continues to bring the Gospel to the Gentiles.

Gospel: Jesus promises peace to his disciples and reiterates his own total obedience to the Father's will.

It is often good and necessary for us to see Jesus and his entire redeeming life and death in the context of the history of humanity, going back to the beginnings. Alienation from God resulted when the first Adam refused to remember the lordship of God over him and his total dependence on God for his life and being. With this alienation from God came the entrance of evil into history.

Jesus, the second Adam, by his total obedience to the Father's will restored humankind to loving union with God. He reconciled humanity to God. Alienation, reconciliation: these two words form the background of Christian theology, Christian liturgy. In today's gospel Jesus goes into detail about the result of his life and death and the obedience that motivated his entire life:

> "Peace" is my farewell to you,
> my peace is my gift to you.

Peace or shalom has many meanings. It is definitely *not* absence of all activity or thought; it is not repose or rest. Essentially peace is a sense of being at one with God, reconciled with him. The peace of Jesus also includes a sense of being forgiven by God. The peace of Jesus also includes absence of fear resulting from obedience to Christ's word: "Do not be distressed or fearful."

It is at the end of today's gospel that Jesus returns again to the principle that motivated his entire life:

> the world must know that I love the Father
> and do as the Father has commanded me.

That is precisely what the first Adam did not do.

The Gospel Verse from Luke (24:46) sums up the entire lifework of Jesus:

> Christ had to suffer and to rise from the dead,
> and so enter into his glory.

We may add: to enter not only into his glory, but to make it possible for us to enter into our glory as well. What Paul says of his having been tortured and left for dead in order to bring the good news to the Gentiles is true of each of us: "We must undergo many trials if we are to enter into the reign of God." What matters is that we see our "many trials"—and they vary for each of us—in the light of what Jesus has done for us. In 2 Cor 4:10 Paul speaks of our sharing in the passion of Christ: "Continually we carry about in our bodies the dying of Jesus, so that in our bodies the life of Jesus may also be revealed."

So,

> All you who fear God, both the great and the small, give praise to him!
> For his salvation and strength have come, the power of Christ, alleluia (Entrance Antiphon).

Jesus has done everything to reconcile us with the Father and make eternal joy and happiness possible for us. What he cannot do is force us to accept it and make his dying and rising our own. So our prayer today is most opportune:

> Father,
> you restored your people to eternal life
> by raising Christ your Son from death.
> Make our faith strong and our hope sure.
> May we never doubt that you will fulfill
> the promises you have made (Opening Prayer).

One final thought that takes us back to Paul's observation about our having to undergo many trials: just as Jesus' sacrifice and death would have been fruitless without its heart of total obedience to the will of the Father, so too our personal passion and eventually our dying. We cannot do what Jesus did: carry a cross; hang on it after three hours of agony; die and rise again as he did. But what we can do is to make our own his total obedience to the Father's will.

> His words are now ours: the world must know that I love the Father and do as the Father has commanded me (Gospel).

287 WEDNESDAY OF THE FIFTH WEEK OF EASTER

READING I Acts 15:1-6
GOSPEL John 15:1-8

Reading I: Because of dissension that disturbed some of the first Christian communities, Paul goes to Jerusalem to consult with other apostles.

Gospel: Jesus compares his Church to a vine and its branches. He is the vine, we are the branches, so intimate is our union with him.

The Church's maternal concern for the well-being of her children, especially those newly born at Easter through baptism, provides the theme for today's Mass. How are these new Christians doing now that the first glow of joy and gratitude has probably worn off? Loving mother that she is, the Church knows how vulnerable all people are and how easy it is to allow the strain and stress of daily life to threaten intimacy with Jesus and cause the diminishing or even the total loss of fervor. Hence our prayer today:

> Father of all holiness,
> guide our hearts to you.
> Keep in the light of your truth
> all those you have freed from the darkness of unbelief (Opening Prayer).

The Church also wants her children to realize how "human" this Church is and has been since its very beginnings, how subject to human failings and disruptive threats from without and from within. Reading I provides this view of the Christian community at Antioch—and just about everywhere else that Paul preached. Paul's entire apostolic career was plagued by some converts from Judaism who were convinced that one could not be a Christian unless one observed all the old Mosaic rules and practices such as ritual circumcision and the dietary laws. They insisted on their conviction even at the risk of destroying the community.

The problem became so acute that the infant Church at Antioch decided to send Paul, Barnabas, and a few others to Jerusalem to place the matters before Peter and the other apostles. This was the setting for the first Church "council," the results of which we shall know in tomorrow's Reading I.

It is in the gospel that the Church's concern for her children becomes specific. Here we see and hear Jesus speaking not only about his personal relationship with each Christian and how they are to maintain that relationship but also the foundation of his Church *as a living community*, with himself as its life principle. "I am the vine, you are the branches," he tells us.

> He who lives in me and I in him,
> will produce abundantly,
> for apart from me you can do nothing.

In a vine or tree the branches that grow out of the trunk are all alive with the same life sap that is in the trunk. So it is with Jesus and us. He is *our* life, our life principle. Because all Christians who are baptized into him live on this one divine life principle, we all constitute one living community, one Church. He is the bond of life making us all one—not only with Christians all over the world, but also with our loved ones who have gone to eternity before us, including those earliest converts of Paul.

The bond between Jesus and his members is a living bond that has to be kept alive, cultivated, and intensified. If the relationship is ignored or taken for granted, it can easily diminish and eventually vanish. So Jesus tells us today:

> Live on in me, as I do in you.
> No more than a branch can bear fruit of itself
> apart from the vine,
> can you bear fruit
> apart from me.

It seems hardly necessary to insist that the best possible way for us to live on in Christ and grow in intimacy with him is through prayer, holy reading, and daily moments of recollection in which we recall all that he has done for us and the love that motivated his entire life, death, and resurrection—and, of course, the Eucharist when possible. Jesus has done everything for us in dying and rising.

Christ has risen and shines upon us, whom he has redeemed by his blood, alleluia (Communion Antiphon).

But he does want our cooperation in responding to his gift. That should not be too difficult if we just remember—remember and celebrate!

288 THURSDAY OF THE FIFTH WEEK OF EASTER

READING I Acts 15:7-21
GOSPEL John 15:9-11

Reading I: The Council of Jerusalem decides that new converts need not submit to Mosaic laws and customs in order to become Christians.

Gospel: Jesus continues his teaching on the primacy of love. He has loved us, so he asks his followers to "Live on in my love."

The Church continues to rejoice in the newborn children to whom she gave spiritual rebirth at their Easter Vigil baptism. As a matter of fact, the Entrance Antiphon actually repeats the response we made to the inspired reading concerning the miraculous passing through the Red Sea—a symbol of baptism—that we heard that night:

> Let us sing to the Lord, he has covered himself in glory! The Lord is my strength, and I praise him: he is the Savior of my life, alleluia.

The Church goes on to pray that the new converts will courageously persevere in living out their new faith in the Opening Prayer.

But, good mother that she is, she provides the converts (and us) with the best possible directives for success in carrying out their goal. She quotes Jesus who called them in the first place:

> My sheep listen to my voice, says the Lord;
> I know them and they follow me (Gospel Verse).

There is no better way of persevering in our vocation as Christians—newborn or veteran—than by listening to Jesus as he speaks to us daily in the gospels. He, of course, knows us. Our problem is to come to know him, for only when we know him as love incarnate will we want to "Live on in [his] love," which definitely includes our observing of his new commandment: that we love one another as he has loved us.

> Lord God,
> by this holy exchange of gifts

you share with us your divine life.
Grant that everything we do
may be directed by the knowledge of your truth (Prayer over the Gifts).

Reading I gives us part two of the decisive Council of Jerusalem to which we were introduced yesterday. We recall the problem: must the Gentile converts observe the Mosaic dietary laws and the law of ritual circumcision in order to become real Christians? After all Jesus and his Mother were Jewish, and so were the apostles. They had observed the Mosaic law, so perhaps it was to be expected that some later Jewish converts should conclude that all Christians must do the same.

The phrase "After much discussion" indicates that there were strong convictions on both sides. Finally it was time for Peter and James to speak. They no longer sound like the simple fishermen who used to test the patience of Jesus with their inability to understand his teaching. Peter touches on the heart of Christian theology when he says: "Our belief is rather that we are saved by the favor of the Lord Jesus and so are they," which is almost a paraphrase of the quote from Paul used in today's Communion Antiphon:

> Christ died for all, so that living men should not live for themselves, but for Christ who died and was raised to life for them.

The description by Paul and Barnabas of how the Lord had worked signs and wonders among the Gentiles helped the cause, and when James, the bishop of Jerusalem who was host of the council, himself a reluctant convert to the view of Peter and Paul, gave his favorable opinion, the argument was over.

Because of the decision of that council we are Christians today. Because of it Jesus and his Church can welcome new converts from any land or race into their arms and hearts without any obligation other than to "Tell his glory among the nations" (Responsorial Psalm) and to "Live on in my love,"—that love which initially summoned them to embrace the faith. Let us sing to the Lord, he has indeed covered himself with glory!

289 FRIDAY OF THE FIFTH WEEK OF EASTER

READING I Acts 15:22-31
GOSPEL John 15:12-17

Reading I: The Jerusalem Council decides to send messengers to Antioch to tell them they need not observe the Mosaic law to be Christians.

Gospel: In today's gospel Jesus calls us his friends and commands us to love one another, "as I have loved you."

Reading I is noteworthy for several reasons, the first being that the Council fathers, "in agreement with the whole Jerusalem church," decided to send messengers to deliver their decision to the Antioch converts. This did not indicate any doubt about Paul's credibility among the Antioch Christians, but it rather pointed to the importance of the decision in the minds of the apostles and elders. They surely helped Paul's and Barnabas' apostolate by calling them "beloved."

What is most fascinating is the wording of the message: "It is the decision of the Holy Spirit, and ours too, not to lay on you any burden beyond that which is strictly necessary." So it is obvious that the Holy Spirit was a precious reality to these first Church fathers. And why not, after the promise of Jesus that he would send the Spirit and their own personal experience of the Holy Spirit's coming into their lives, their minds, and hearts on Pentecost? These people are well aware of their identity!

We are members of that same Spirit-filled Church, and we continue to celebrate the death and resurrection of Jesus in *this* year of our Lord.

> May our celebration of Christ's death and resurrection
> guide us to salvation (Opening Prayer).

We can add: Guide us to the fullness of life in this world and help us to become more aware of the presence of the Holy Spirit in *our* lives.

Naturally the best context for celebrating the death and resurrection of Jesus is our remembering of the fact that five weeks ago today was Good Friday.

> The Lamb who was slain is worthy to receive strength and divinity, wisdom and power and honor, alleluia (Entrance Antiphon).

But the bothersome question persists: does he receive all that homage from our world, from the newborn Christians, from me?

One hesitates to moralize about the act of love on the part of Jesus, but, on the other hand, the very texts of the Mass cry out for some comparison between the reality of our Christian life and the ideal response to this divine act of love that ought to rise from our determined and grateful hearts.

The Christian life is—or ought to be—growth in a loving relationship with Jesus, who today calls us his friends. Friendship has been called one of God's greatest gifts. That is just ordinary friendship between two persons who have learned to respect, esteem, and confide in one another. The life of a person without friends is inconceivably dull—and tragic. But how much more tragic the life of a person who was once intimate with Christ and then loses the relationship. Friendship can never be taken for granted. Like the love between wife and husband, it has to be maintained and cultivated by a confiding kind of conversation, or it fades.

This is surely the case with our friendship with Jesus, as well as with those fellow members of his body he speaks about today when he tells us:

> This is my commandment:
> love one another
> as I have loved you.

We need not argue about whether or not anyone can command love, since love has to be a free act. But love can certainly be helped along both by the greatest of all lovers, Jesus, and by those who lend their hearts to him so that he can love in and through them. Which is why we pray:

> Lord,
> may this eucharist,
> which we have celebrated in memory of your Son,
> help us to grow in love (Prayer after Communion).

In a word the key to all love is Jesus and our never-ending remembering of how much he loved us.

> The man who died on the cross has risen from the dead, and has won back our lives from death, alleluia (Communion Antiphon).

290 SATURDAY OF THE FIFTH WEEK OF EASTER

READING I Acts 16:1-10
GOSPEL   John 15:18-21

Reading I: The author of Acts continues his narrative of the activities of Paul and Timothy throughout the Mideast.

Gospel: Jesus warns his disciples that they will be harried by the world because they bear his name.

Five weeks ago tonight we celebrated the resurrection of Jesus; new converts were received into the Church, and we all renewed our baptismal commitment to Jesus Christ. The memory lingers on and finds various expressions in today's Mass. Thus the Entrance Antiphon states:

> In baptism we have died with Christ, and we have risen to new life in him, because we believed in the power of God
> who raised him from the dead, alleluia.

If the enthusiasm and joy of that blessed night have given way to the drabness of daily life, we need this reminder of the real meaning of our baptism: we died with Christ, we rose with him, alleluia!

We have also lived long enough since Holy Saturday to realize our need for the "unceasing care" we pray for in the Opening Prayer:

> Loving Father,
> through our rebirth in baptism
> you give us your life and promise immortality.
> By your *unceasing care,*
> guide our steps toward the life of glory (italics mine).

Now, too, we may know something about the reality of Christ's prediction of being hated by the world just because we belong to him and claim to be his followers:

> "If you find that the world hates you,
> know it has hated me before you.
> If you belonged to the world,
> it would love you as its own;
> the reason it hates you
> is that you do not belong to the world" (Gospel).

Living in this culture in this country, we have probably not experienced a great deal of outright hatred or harassment—pity perhaps and a bit of scorn at being so naive as to take seriously a man who lived two thousand years ago and was so simple-minded as to expect his disciples to love one another "as I have loved you" (John 15:12). What we have experienced most of all is probably indifference, and that can be just as hard to accept as outright hatred. Someone has said that the opposite of love is not so much hatred as indifference.

How exact is the reason Jesus gives for the kind of treatment we can expect from the world:

> All this they will do to you because of my name,
> *for they know nothing of him who sent me* (italics mine).

But maybe they are not entirely at fault for knowing nothing of the Father and little more about Jesus Christ. It could be that we Christians are more to blame than they. If the Christian ideal of personal caring for others (following the example of Jesus), of living for others, is not evident in our lives, and above all if we fail to try (at least) to put into practice that mutual love for one another that Jesus wanted more than anything else, we are being unworthy of the choice Jesus made of us to be his followers.

The Communion Antiphon reminds us again of our responsibility:

> Father, I pray for them: may they be one in us, so that the world may believe it was you who sent me, alleluia.

A natural, cultivated, and honest love and respect of Christian for Christian—for all Christians, but especially those in our family, our parish, or our community form the most powerful missionary thrust there is. It is the strongest argument for the genuineness of Christianity.

But maybe there is a still stronger argument: it is *joy* in the attitudes and even the faces of those whom Jesus has chosen to be his very own. But life is hard, and joy is fragile, so we pray:

> Lord,
> watch over those you have saved in Christ.
> May we who are redeemed by his suffering and death
> always rejoice in his resurrection,
> for he is Lord for ever and ever (Prayer after Communion).

May our Amen to that plea be loud and clear!

56 SIXTH SUNDAY OF EASTER Cycle A

READING I Acts 8:5-8, 14-17 READING II 1 Peter 3:15-18
GOSPEL John 14:15-21

Reading I: We read and hear the account of Philip's preaching in Samaria and the calling down of the Holy Spirit by the imposing of hands of Peter and John.

Reading II: Peter gives practical advice for Christian living and reminds us again of Christ's having died for our sins once for all.

Gospel: Jesus tells us that the only way to demonstrate our love for him is by loving one another. He promises to send the Holy Spirit.

> Ever-living God,
> help us to celebrate our joy
> in the resurrection of the Lord
> and to express in our lives
> the love we celebrate (Opening Prayer).

We probably seldom if ever think of celebrating love, but this prayer tells us to celebrate not only love but joy as well. Actually we have been celebrating love ever since we celebrated the birth of Jesus last Christmas, and we just finished celebrating his death and resurrection, the crowning act of his love for us. We continue celebrating that love today, and we look forward with eagerness to the outpouring of divine love in the coming feast of Pentecost.

Reading I concludes with a fascinating bit of information: after Philip had proclaimed the Messiah in Samaria and won many converts, Peter and John go there, impose hands on the converts, and "they received the Holy Spirit." It is possible that not many Catholics know that the imposing of hands has always been the sign of calling down the Holy Spirit and that the imposing of hands is now part of the ritual of every sacrament. Recall what the priest says when he uses any of the four Eucharistic Prayers, for example:

> Let your Spirit come upon these gifts to make them holy,
> so that they may become for us
> the body and blood of our Lord, Jesus Christ (Eucharistic Prayer II).

> Shout joyfully to God, all you on earth,
> Hear now, all you who fear God,
> while I declare
> what he has done for me (Responsorial Psalm).

What God has done for me and all of us is to give us his Son Jesus as our Savior, our guide, our life. And this Jesus, in addition to dying and rising for us, gives us a way of life:

> If you love me
> and obey the commands I give you,
> I will ask the Father
> and he will give you another Paraclete—
> to be with you always: the Spirit of truth. . . .
> He who obeys the commandments
> he has from me
> is the man who loves me (Gospel).

We know, of course, what his commandments are: "Love one another as I have loved you." Jesus calls this his new commandment.

It may be possible that we hear too much about love in these pre-Pentecost Sunday Masses. Perhaps the problem is that we hear always the same old things, or that we have tried and failed to practice Christ's commandment, or that we have tried and been rebuffed. We have heard often enough that *loving* is not the same as *liking* and being with someone we admire and cherish. (The problem is that most of us not only want to be *loved* but also *liked*.) We have also heard that loving one another or another person is willing (not just wishing) the good and the well-being of another. That may be the real secret of heeding Christ's commandment. Or again, it may help to seek out the good in another person and that person's way of life.

Eventually it seems that all human efforts fail, and we are forced to admit our helplessness, our absolute need for divine help. It is that divine help that we pray for and that Jesus promises in these Sundays immediately preceding Pentecost.

> The Father will send you the Holy Spirit, to be with you for ever (Communion Antiphon).

That promise will be fulfilled, it has to be, because Jesus made it, but only on condition that we admit our need and open our whole being to welcome the Holy Spirit, who is Divine Love in person. So we repeat:

> Ever-living God,
> help us to celebrate our joy
> in the resurrection of the Lord
> and to express in our lives
> the love we celebrate (Opening Prayer).

Could it be that joy is the real secret of loving and the real secret of joy is remembering all that Jesus has done for us? So, Lord, help us to remember, so as to rejoice, so as to love!

57 SIXTH SUNDAY OF EASTER Cycle B

READING I Acts 10:25-26, 34-35, 44-48   READING II 1 John 4:7-10
GOSPEL   John 15:9-17

Reading I: We hear of a dramatic opening of Christianity to the Gentiles and how the Holy Spirit comes upon Peter's audience.

Reading II: John tells us that we must love one another because love is of God and no one who knows not love knows anything of God.

Gospel: Again we hear Jesus' commandment that we love one another as he has loved us.

The resurrection of Jesus was so great an event that by our own power alone we are incapable of celebrating it as it deserves. So we pray:

> Ever-living God,
> help us to celebrate our joy
> in the resurrection of the Lord (Opening Prayer).

Celebrating an event is the best possible way to keep the event alive in our hearts and minds, but more is needed than the memory of the event. The death and resurrection of Jesus demands an ongoing transformation of our lives. Our prayer concludes:

> help us . . .
> to express in our lives
> the love we celebrate.

Today we celebrate joy and we celebrate love. Love and joy belong together in every Christian heart, and the bond uniting joy and love is Jesus in his love for us. Love and joy are what this Mass is all about. At the Last Supper Jesus said:

> Live on in my love [a beautiful echo of our opening prayer]. . . .
> All this I tell you
> that my joy may be yours
> and your joy may be complete.

And how is our joy made complete? "This is my commandment: love one another as I have loved you." We know from experience that to love others as Jesus loves us—that is, to the death—is impossible by our own strength alone. But we are not, never have been, and never will be alone. Jesus promises:

> The Father will send you the Holy Spirit, to be with you for ever (Communion Antiphon).

That is not an empty promise!

But talking about love and actual loving are two different things. We need to know how to love, and for that we need living exemplars, not forgetting that the life of Jesus is the best example of all. We are all aware of people around us who prove their love for others by giving themselves to them. Newspapers and TV tell us daily about women and men who are unashamed of demonstrating their love to the world. The fact is that they *care* for people, especially the poor, the little ones, the helpless and homeless, the aged. Most large cities have their houses of hospitality and soup kitchens that are always in need of help.

It may not be possible for all of us to become active in this kind of caring, but it is possible, with the help of the Holy Spirit, to show our love in other ways.

> Anyone who loves me
> will be true to my word,
> and my Father will love him;
> we will come to him   (Gospel Verse).

Holiness Is Wholeness is the title of a book by the German priest Josef Goldbrunner. The idea of the book is that wholeness of personality is possible only by our becoming and remaining loving, caring persons. It is in loving that we attain the highest degree of our humanity, holiness. At the beginning of life we are incomplete human beings. The only road to fulfillment is the road of loving and caring *and*, it must be added, allowing ourselves *to be loved and cared for by others*. If any of us amount to anything, if we have friends who are attracted to us, if we are respected, most often we have to attribute the credit to those who have trusted us, believed in us. And the one who has believed in us most of all is Jesus. His love is undying, it is forgiving, it is merciful, it is everlasting.

Whatever wholeness and completeness we have has to be shared if it is to remain our own and continue to expand. We can never take a vacation from loving, caring, and allowing ourselves to be loved and cared for. We have all been brought to fulfillment by others, especially by Jesus, and so we have to carry on in the same divine way.

> Beloved,
> let us love one another
> because love is of God;
> everyone who loves is begotten of God
> and has knowledge of God (Reading II).

So loving and caring have to become the life principle for us all, a *conscious* life principle, one that is never out of our minds or our attitudes. Since we so often fail, we pray:

> Lord, ...
> Make us worthy of your sacraments of love
> by granting us your forgiveness (Prayer over the Gifts).

We know from experience how often we fail to live up to Christ's expectations of us in the matter of loving one another; we know how powerless we have been and are in loving as Jesus loved; we know how very much we need help, and so does he. This is why two weeks from today he will send us his Holy Spirit who will remain with us to love in and through us, but again only if we realize our need and are willing to allow the Spirit permanent residence in our hearts, our lives.

> Speak out with a voice of joy; let it be heard to the ends of the earth: the Lord has set his people free (Entrance Antiphon).

He has set us free to love. It is up to us to retain and grow in that freedom.

58 SIXTH SUNDAY OF EASTER — Cycle C

READING I Acts 15:1-2, 22-29
READING II Rev 21:10-14, 22-23
GOSPEL John 14:23-29

Reading I: We listen to an account of the Council of Jerusalem, the reason why it was called and its decisions.

Reading II: The author of Revelation allows us to see a vision of the Church at the end of time, the Lord God and the Lamb of God will be the temple of the new Holy City.

Gospel: Jesus promises his disciples peace and lays down the law by which his disciples can be known: love for him demonstrated by love for one's neighbor.

Today Jesus announces to the apostles and to all the world:

> "Peace" is my farewell to you,
> my peace is my gift to you.

When he appeared to that same group of apostles the night of his resurrection, he greeted them with the words: "Peace be with you." Peace may well be the first fruits of the resurrection. Of course we all remember Christmas and the angels' announcement: "Peace on earth to men of good will." The child born to Mary was called the Prince of Peace.

Peacemaking was Christ's entire life; it was the essential element of his message, his good news. "Blest too the peacemakers; they shall be called sons of God," (Matt 5:9) he tells us in the Beatitudes, which might be called the charter of Christianity. Peace—reconciling people to God, reconciling people to people, doing away with enmities of all kinds—was Christ's lifetime work; it is still the lifework of his Church. "My peace is my gift to you," he tells his apostles, his Church today. Peace is a gift that demands sharing. All of Christian history, all of our own experience, tell us that it is not easy.

What is peace for Christ? The Hebrew word is *shalom* which is still used as a greeting between friends; it is an expression of good-will. *The Dictionary of the Bible* by Father John McKenzie says there is so much content to the word *shalom* that no single English word can really render it.

Shalom signifies a general completeness and perfection, a condition in which nothing is lacking; it is perfect well-being that is much more than mere prosperity. Peace for Christ is not absence of trouble or worry or concern. It does not mean avoiding or escaping hard decisions. It is refusing to let life's problems overcome one. It involves the confident ability to come to terms with life and all its problems.

In its deepest meaning peace can be said to be a sense of life's wholeness and purposefulness, a sense of spiritual soundness, the understanding at the deepest level of one's being that *you are somebody* in the eyes of the self-giving God.

The peace that Jesus gives is not the peace that the world gives; it is definitely not the peace that results from vast supplies of nuclear arms. Such a feeling of peace is all too fragile, much too temporary. It is not a lull between wars and battles. Paul tells us: "Let us, then, make it our aim to work for peace and to strengthen one another" (Rom 14:19).

The enemy of peace is destructive dissension, the kind described in Reading I today. It was caused by Christian converts from Judaism who insisted on imposing the obligations of the old Mosaic law on recent Christian converts from paganism. Tragically dissension of some kind or other has haunted Christianity and individual parishes and communities from that day to our own. "Has Christ, then, been divided into parts?" Paul once asked the Christians in Corinth (1 Cor 1:13). If Jesus could say, "Blessed are the peacemakers," we can imagine what he thinks of those who cause dissension among his own.

"Peace" is my farewell to you,
my peace is my gift to you.

Jesus is simply offering us the wholeness of life which our hearts crave. But again peace given by Jesus to us has to be shared; it demands a response. It is like love. Like love it also has to be made, created. Willingness to share Christ's peace is part of the symbolism of the Sign of Peace at Mass. Our first obligation is to be willing to receive Christ's peace both from him and from one another. Then perhaps we shall learn how to give peace, to make peace, and to share peace.

Making and sharing peace demands heroism. For that we know we cannot do it alone. We badly need, we always need, the presence of the Holy Spirit in our lives, that same Holy Spirit who "presided" at the Jerusalem Council ("It is the decision of the Holy Spirit, and ours too" the Apostles said). With our world as threatened as it is by war and terrorism, there has never been a greater need for openness of all Christian hearts in welcoming the Holy Spirit whom Jesus promises to send us two weeks from today.

291 MONDAY OF THE SIXTH WEEK OF EASTER

READING I Acts 16:11-15
GOSPEL John 15:26§16:4

Reading I: Today Paul and Luke are at Philippi where Paul converts Lydia and accepts her invitation to make his headquarters at her house.

Gospel: Jesus promises to send the Holy Spirit upon his apostles so that they may be able to bear witness to him. They will be persecuted.

God of mercy,
may our celebration of your Son's resurrection
help us to experience its effect in our lives (Opening Prayer).

We may well wonder what exactly is the effect of Christ's resurrection. Paul says in Romans that by our baptism into Christ's death we are buried with him so that just as Christ was raised from the dead by the glory of the Father, we too *might live a new life* (see Rom 6:5).

We pray, therefore, that the newness of Christ's risen body will remain with us, that we will experience it and rejoice in and be enthusiastic about our new condition. Implicit in the Opening Prayer (and in Romans) is the notion that, having been freed from sin, we not only remain in that blessed condition but grow in ever-increasing intimacy with Christ. "In the same way, you must consider yourselves dead to sin but alive for God in Christ Jesus" (Rom 6:11).

In Reading I we come for the first time to the "we" sections of Acts. This change would seem to indicate that the author Luke is now working and traveling with Paul. His description of the conversion of the lady Lydia is theologically exact: "the Lord opened her heart to accept what Paul was saying." So being converted is much more than a matter of being convinced in mind of the reasonableness of the Gospel. True and lasting conversion results only when the truth and its divine author take possession of and warm our hearts—our entire being. It is not hard to imagine Luke smiling when he writes (after Lydia invites them to stay in her house): "She managed to prevail on us."

The receptivity of the Philippians to the Gospel and the wonderful personality of Lydia prompts the Church to respond with the psalm verse: "The Lord loves his people." It is a lovely phrase that not only states an easily forgotten fact but also presents a challenge to us to continue to deserve the privilege of giving joy to God.

For that we need help, and Jesus promises it to us in the gospel:

> When the Paraclete comes,
> the Spirit of truth who comes from the Father—
> and whom I myself will send from the Father—
> he will bear witness on my behalf.
> You must bear witness as well.

The apostles at the Last Supper needed to hear those reassuring words:

> I have told you all this
> to keep your faith from being shaken.

Jesus tells them that, and he goes on to predict the sufferings they will have to undergo in their apostolate.

Our need for reassurance in our faith is even greater, for most of us live in a distraction-filled world. The apostles had only one vocation, to preach the Gospel. Most modern Christians have the vocation of living the Gospel and being wives, husbands, religious, and priests as well. Then there are the vocations imposed on them by their various professions. It is just not very easy to be able to experience the effect of the resurrection in our lives.

So we need all the help we can get. We need the Holy Spirit. We need him for the progress of that ongoing conversion that must characterize our lives as Christians. So we can take the lady Lydia as our counsellor and *prevail upon* the Lord to send the Spirit into our hearts at the coming feast of Pentecost. In the Opening Prayer we pray for the ability to experience the *effect* of the resurrection. In the Prayer after Communion we pray that

> by these Easter mysteries [the Lord will]
> bring us to the glory of the resurrection.

Such a marvellous goal can only be accomplished in us by the power of the Holy Spirit.

292 TUESDAY OF THE SIXTH WEEK OF EASTER

READING I Acts 16:22-34
GOSPEL John 16:5-11

Reading I: The Philippians turn against Paul and Silas and imprison them, but they are miraculously rescued, and their jailer is converted.

Gospel: Jesus tries to comfort the apostles by promising to send the Holy Spirit upon them.

> Your right hand saves me, O Lord (Responsorial Psalm).

This short psalm verse describes exactly what God did for Paul, for Paul's jailer, for those baptized last Easter, and for each and every one of us who are Christian.

> God our Father,
> may we look forward with hope to our resurrection,
> for you have made us your sons and daughters,
> and restored the joy of our youth (Opening Prayer).

It is God, and he alone, who saves.

Paul's jailer, having witnessed the extraordinary events of Paul's deliverance, asks: "Men, what must I do to be saved?" It is a typical question for most human beings, including many Catholics, who ought to know better. Everyone seems to think that religion and salvation consists in our doing things for God in order to win his favor. Paul says simply: "Believe in the Lord Jesus and you will be saved, and all your household."

Believing for Paul is much more than accepting doctrines that we cannot fully understand. When Paul says, "Believe in the Lord Jesus," he really means: "Put your whole trust in him, place your life in his hands!" He means above all: "Be willing to receive Christ's love, the reconciliation with God, the *salvation* Jesus won for you by his death and resurrection." If you really want to *do* something, then just be grateful:

> I will give thanks to you, O Lord,
> with all my heart (Responsorial Psalm).

The Last Supper was an essential part of the whole process of salvation, and for the last few weeks John has been sharing with us his memory of Jesus' farewell message to his apostles. Part of Christ's suffering must surely have been the obvious anguish of his beloved group of friends at that meal. We have to admit that what he tells them does not immediately lessen their pain. For that they have to wait for the fulfillment of his promise to send them the Holy Spirit. Today Jesus says:

> Because I have had all this to say to you,
> you are overcome with grief.
> Yet I tell you the sober truth:
> It is much better for you that I go.
> If I fail to go,
> the Paraclete will never come to you,
> whereas if I go,
> I will send him to you.

It is obvious that for Jesus the sending of the Holy Spirit was of the utmost importance, actually just as essential to the fullness of redemption as his own life, his preaching, his death and resurrection. The history of the fulfillment of his promise as related in Acts proves how right he was. We will also know how right he was when in less than two weeks we celebrate and make our own the coming of the Holy Spirit that he promised. We will hopefully also come to know that our celebration of that coming this year is as crucial for us as it was for the apostles.

The apostles probably did not understand Jesus' words about the Holy Spirit's task of proving

> the world wrong
> about sin,
> about justice,
> about condemnation

any better than we do. Commentators have a hard time explaining what Jesus actually meant. We can settle for the note in the *New American Bible* that "[the Paraclete] leads believers to see . . . that the basic sin of men was and is their refusal to believe in Jesus; . . . that it is the prince of this world, Satan, who has been condemned through Jesus' death." Now perhaps we can understand how right Paul was when he told his jailer: "Believe in the Lord Jesus and you will be saved." That advice is as fresh and necessary today as it was when it came forth from Paul's mouth and heart.

> Your kindness, O Lord, endures forever;
> forsake not the work of your hands (Responsorial Psalm).

293 WEDNESDAY OF THE SIXTH WEEK OF EASTER

READING I Acts 17:15, 22–18:1
GOSPEL   John 16:12-15

Reading I: Paul loses the attention of the Athenians when he mentions the resurrection of Jesus.

Gospel: Jesus tells the apostles at the Last Supper that the Holy Spirit will guide them to all truth.

The Lord says, I have chosen you from the world to go and bear fruit that will last, alleluia (Communion Antiphon).

These words of Jesus, first heard by the apostles at the Last Supper, were surely true of Paul. But they are true of us as well. We also have been chosen to be Christ's disciples, and by leading the Christian life in whatever vocation to which he has called us, we are to be witnesses to Christ in the world and spread the knowledge of his name wherever we go (see Entrance Antiphon).

Today's first reading shows how shrewd Paul was in adapting the Christian revelation to the thinking and mentality of his hearers, thus providing us with an essential lesson on the need to adapt the Gospel to the culture and education of prospective modern converts. The Greeks were unlike any other people Paul had thus far encountered. They were well educated in literature, mathematics, and above all philosophy. St. Thomas Aquinas, the Catholic Church's most illustrious theologian, knew the works of their great philosopher Aristotle and drew much inspiration from them. Another great Greek philosopher, Plato, had a great influence on the teaching of St. Augustine.

So today we see and hear Paul appealing to the men of Athens on their own ground, both literally and intellectually. His argument was simply that the existence of God is to be deduced from looking at the world around us. Later in his letter to the Romans, Paul will formulate his doctrine clearly: "Since the creation of the world, invisible realities, God's eternal power and divinity, have become visible, *recognized through the things he has made*" (Rom 1:20) (italics mine).

Here in Athens Paul tells his hearers that God not only gives existence to the universe and the world, but that he also gives life. He recognizes that their knowledge of God derived from reason is groping and inadequate. Hopefully, however, they will find him, since "he is not really far from any one of us."

We can judge how close the Greek poets were to divine truth when Paul quotes from their writings, "In him [God] we live and move and have our being." This phrase, if we make it part of our consciousness, can become a beautiful prayer which can bring us close to God and help us grow in love. Indeed for us as for the Greeks, "Heaven and earth are filled with your glory" (Responsorial Psalm).

Despite his ability to adapt his message to their mentality, Paul is only partially successful, and he loses most of his audience when he passes from philosophy to revelation and mentions "one [Jesus] whom he [God] has endorsed in the sight of all by raising him from the dead." Some sneered and others said: "We must hear you on this topic some other time." Paul leaves them, and there is no evidence that he ever returned to Athens. But there can be no doubt that those who heard him advanced more than a little in their longing search for God.

By hearing Paul and absorbing his convictions, we too can come closer to the goal to which we have been called: that of witnessing to Christ in our own way and environment. When we reflect back on our lack of interest in witnessing, we realize more and more how very much we need the Holy Spirit whom Jesus will send to us on Pentecost, now only ten days away.

> When he comes, . . .
> being the Spirit of truth
> he will guide you to all truth.

> Merciful Father,
> may these mysteries give us new purpose
> and bring us to a new life in you (Prayer after Communion).

May these mysteries also intensify our burning desire for the coming of the Spirit into our hearts!

294 THURSDAY OF THE SIXTH WEEK OF EASTER

(This Mass is celebrated in countries where the feast of the Ascension is transferred to the following Sunday.)

READING I Acts 18:1-8
GOSPEL John 16:16-20

Reading I: In Corinth Paul worked at his trade as a tentmaker and on the sabbath he led discussions about Jesus in the synagogue.

Gospel: Jesus tells the apostles that he will leave them in a short while but soon after that they will see him again.

The Entrance Antiphon of today's Mass might well be its best theme. It takes us back to the Exodus of God's people from Egyptian slavery.

> When you walked at the head of your people, O God, and lived with them on their journey, the earth shook at your presence.

The key words are "lived with them on their journey." See the Book of Exodus for details.

Well, God's living with his people did not cease back then. He is still doing it, and *we* are now that people. Jesus tells us in the Communion Antiphon: "I, the Lord, am with you always, until the end of the world." He made that promise after his work on earth was finished and he was about to ascend to his Father (see Matt 28:20). He leaves but is still with us—still with his Church, still with each of us, his members.

We too are on a journey, an exodus, on our way to our promised land. At times the way and the obstacles and detours seem impossible to overcome, and we come close to despair (as often happened to the Jews in their Exodus), and those are the times when we have to remind ourselves of Jesus' promise to be with us always—always, no matter how we might stray from the main highway.

Jesus has earned our confidence and our trust. We may doubt at weak moments, but he even anticipated those moments of fear and concern about the future when he spoke to the apostles (and to us):

> Within a short time you will lose sight of me,
> but soon after that you shall see me again (Gospel).

He said that at the Last Supper, and when he rose from the dead, they realized how right he was.

Our problem may be that we do not experience Jesus' presence as the apostles did during their years with him and during that period after his resurrection. Ours is strictly a life of faith. But that is the way it is and always will be for the Christian. Christianity is a life of faith, or it is not Christianity.

Paul lived on faith in Jesus and love for him. He was not always successful in his preaching, as we have heard in the readings from Acts during this Easter season. He tried hard to convert his fellow Jews to Christ, but he received the greatest opposition from those who had become Christian but refused to give up their attachment to the Old Law, insisting that even the Gentiles who became Christian had to observe it. Today's Reading I is a typical example of that kind of opposition. Little wonder that he shook out his garments in protest and exclaimed: "Your blood be on your own heads. I am not to blame! From now on, I will turn to the Gentiles."

Few of us run into that kind of opposition. Most of our trouble comes from within. Our Prayer after Communion today fits our condition perfectly:

> Almighty and ever-living Lord,
> you restored us to life
> by raising Christ from death.
> Strengthen us by this Easter sacrament;
> may we feel its saving power in our daily life.

So, let us all get back on the road to our promised land with deepest confidence in him who walks at our head.

59 ASCENSION

READING I Acts 1:1-11 **READING II** Eph 1:17-23
GOSPEL Matt 28:16-20

Reading I: Jesus speaks for the last time to his apostles, promises to send the Holy Spirit, and sends them out to the whole world to be his witnesses.

Reading II: Paul prays for the Ephesians that they may have a spirit of wisdom and insight to know God clearly and to know the great hope to which God has called them.

Gospel: Matthew relates Christ's final commission of Jesus to the apostles before Christ ascends. Jesus promises to be with them always.

Jesus' work on earth is finished. He ascends to his "Father's right hand." But is the work finished? What does ascend mean? Is he really gone from the apostles, from us? It may well be that the very language of this feast obscures its deep and true meaning for us. We hear the language and think: he ascended, he went up into a cloud—the Scriptural symbol of God's dwelling place—so he is gone, gone from us, but can this be true?

Yes, it is true, if we consider only his original bodily presence. But we believe that already in his resurrection he entered upon a new, completely unprecedented manner of existence. Time and space no longer placed any restrictions upon him. He simply appeared to his followers through locked doors; he ate, drank, and conversed with them.

His ascension may well have been an advancement or a perfecting of that new existence of his. Now he no longer appears in a bodily form, but he has by no means departed from them in his real being as God's Son. Otherwise how do we explain his words at the end of today's gospel: "And know that I am with you always, until the end of the world"? He is with us, with the Church. It is a real presence, not just figurative language. It is truth. The ascension is not an end, but a beginning, the beginning of a new manner of Christ's activity among the apostles and in us his Church. The Preface of this feast expresses this fact so beautifully:

> [He] has passed beyond our sight,
> not to abandon us but to be our hope.
> Christ is the beginning, the head of the Church;
> where he has gone, we hope to follow.

It is not easy for us earthbound creatures to even come close to understanding the meaning of this new kind of presence Jesus now maintains with us. How can he be away and still be here? We really need the prayer that Paul composed for the Ephesians: "May the God of our Lord Jesus Christ . . . grant you a spirit of wisdom and insight to know him clearly. May he enlighten your innermost vision that you may know the great hope to which he has called you." What is that hope? It is eternal happiness at the end of our lives, but much more. It is the hope that the work begun by Jesus in his life on earth may continue and prosper in his Church now and always and that each of us may personally carry out whatever share of that work he has decreed for us.

So the ascension is one of the most enlightening events in the long process of the world's redemption begun when Jesus was born into our human family. He has laid the groundwork by his preaching, his death, and his resurrection. Now the work goes on, *and we are part of it.* Is not this what the angels had in mind when they saw the apostles gazing up into the heavens, trying to follow Jesus as he ascends? "Men of Galilee, . . . why do you stand here looking up to the skies? This Jesus who has been taken from you will return, just as you saw him go up into the heavens." In other words, there is work to be done; get going!

Then there is Jesus' own command:

> go, therefore, and make disciples of all the nations. . . .
> I am with you always, until the end of the world!

If we love Christ, the spread of the gospel has to be close to all our hearts. We are not all called to be missionaries, but each of us can help carry on that work by our prayers, by our sufferings offered for the missions and missionaries, and by whatever contributions we can make. Missionaries depend on their fellow Christians to help them carry on their and Christ's work.

We believe that the liturgy makes present *for us* the entire life, work, death, and resurrection of Jesus in every Mass, in every feast. This means that the feasts are not journeys into the past. They are *now*. We celebrate the Ascension *today*. And all that it meant for the apostles is meant for us as well.

There is something else in the picture of the apostles' gazing up into heaven. Think of the desire for Jesus in their hearts, the yearning, the hunger to possess him always and to be possessed by him. Sharing in that desire for Jesus, making it our own, may well be the greatest grace that this feast has for us today.

In today's Prayer after Communion we cry out:

> Father,
> in this Eucharist
> we touch the divine life you give to the world.
> Help us to follow Christ with love
> to eternal life where he is Lord for ever and ever.

May the Holy Spirit whom Jesus will send us on Pentecost fill us all with an overflowing love and hunger for our beloved Jesus!

But now let us all get to work and do all that we can to carry to completion the task that Jesus has given into our hands.

Note:
The readings, prayers, and antiphons for this feast are the same for Cycles A, B, and C except for the three gospels of Matthew, Mark, and Luke. Each of these gospels centers on the ascension of the Lord, but in each case this truth is introduced by an additional insight into the entire redemptive work of Jesus. Thus Matthew mentions a mountain in Galilee—Matthew seems to like the symbolism of mountains;

writing for the Jews, he tries to compare Jesus with the great Jewish hero Moses. Mark emphasizes Jesus' signs (especially that of healing) that will accompany the apostles' preaching. Luke points out how the triumph of Jesus was the inevitable consequence of his having had to suffer and die in order to arrive at his glorification. Each gospel gives an insight into how the apostles carried out their commission, and also each records the important promise of Jesus that he would be with them always until the end of the world.

295 FRIDAY OF THE SIXTH WEEK OF EASTER

READING I Acts 18:9-18
GOSPEL   John 16:20-23

Reading I: In Corinth Paul runs into violent opposition from the Judaizers who accuse him of influencing people to worship God in ways that are against the law.

Gospel: Still at the Last Supper, Jesus promises the apostles that the grief they feel will soon be turned into joy.

After yesterday's "high" it seems a little unreal to return to the quiet celebrating of the Easter season we have been engaged in the last six weeks. But that is the way life is. Either extreme—all highs or all normals—would be boring and unnatural. Besides there are plenty of echoes of the ascension in today's Mass. There are also echoes of Good Friday, as we might expect. What a contrast between that day and the feast of the Ascension we rejoiced in yesterday! But even in the Entrance Antiphon there is a hint of ultimate triumph:

> By your blood, O Lord, you have redeemed us from every tribe and tongue, from every nation and people: you have made us into the kingdom of God, alleluia.

The Opening Prayer brings together the entire redeeming act of Jesus—his death and resurrection, the ascension, his final coming in glory along with the hope of all Christians, especially those who were baptized on Holy Saturday night:

> may he clothe with immortality
> all who have been born again in baptism.
>
> Christ had to suffer and rise from the dead,
> and so enter into his glory.

So the Gospel Verse reminds us. But if Christ had to suffer to enter into his glory, so too the Christian and especially the apostle of Christ. Reading I tells how that divine principle was verified in the life of Paul. It may or may not seem strange that the ones who made life most miserable for Paul were not the pagans but his own countrymen, particularly those Hebrews who had become Christians and who insisted that all converts should practice the ancient Jewish law and customs. They hated Paul because he insisted that Jesus had redeemed us and that there was therefore no need for anyone to try to redeem himself by obeying all kinds of rules that were not essential to Christianity.

Usually the Responsorial Psalm responds in kind to the first reading, but today it remembers yesterday's feast instead:

> God is king of all the earth.
> All you peoples, clap your hands,
> shout to God with cries of gladness. . . .
> God mounts his throne amid shouts of joy. . . .
> Sing praise to God, sing praise,
> sing praise to our king, sing praise.

Remembering yesterday, that is not a difficult command to obey.

Remembering also the joys still to come, the Good Friday theme is again very evident. Jesus is still trying to calm the fears and dread of the apostles at the Last Supper. He tells them:

> you will weep and mourn
> while the world rejoices;
> you will grieve for a time,
> but your grief will be turned into joy . . .
> you are sad for a time, but I shall see you again;
> then your hearts will rejoice
> with a joy no one can take from you.

Knowing by hindsight what actually happened when Jesus was arrested, tried, crowned with thorns, and nailed to a cross, it is not difficult to understand that Jesus was only partially successful in his efforts to calm their fears. With that same hindsight and the realization of how Jesus actually did triumph over death, his words really ought to be more applicable to us than to the apostles.

> When a woman is in labor
> she is sad that her time has come.
> When she has borne her child,
> she no longer remembers her pain
> for joy that a man has been born into the world.

We are that woman, each one of us. We are in labor with sickness, old age, distress of all kinds, sorrows and losses, family troubles, joblessness, and so on and on, oftentimes bringing us close to despair. Is it possible for us to take Jesus at his word here? Is there any light at all in the surrounding darkness? There is for those who have faith and for those who remember that Christ had to suffer and die to enter into his glory. Is there any reason why any human, above all, any of his followers should get by without traveling that same way?

296 SATURDAY OF THE SIXTH WEEK OF EASTER

READING I Acts 18:23-28
GOSPEL John 16:23-28

Reading I: We hear about a remarkable Jewish convert named Apollos who fearlessly proclaims his faith in Jesus in the synagogue at Ephesus.

Gospel: Jesus tells the apostles how to pray and also that they are loved by the Father because they have loved him.

From now until Pentecost the liturgy reflects both Jesus' resurrection and his ascension, with a growing anticipation of the coming of the Holy Spirit as well. Today is Saturday, so there is even a recollection of the Holy Saturday vigil with its strong emphasis on baptism:

> You are a people God claims as his own, to praise him who called you out of darkness into his marvelous light, alleluia (Entrance Antiphon).

Even though the Opening Prayer refers to what happened at Jesus' ascension, we can surely make it our own now:

> Father,
> at your Son's ascension into heaven
> you promised to send the Holy Spirit on your apostles.
> You filled them with heavenly wisdom:
> fill us also with the gift of your Spirit.

We are baptized, members of Christ, alive with his life, but without the Holy Spirit we can be just as dull and lacking in understanding of Jesus and our Christian life as were the apostles before Pentecost. We never have enough of the Spirit. More, more, more, is our constant prayer.

The chief character in today's Reading I is not Paul but Apollos, a learned Jew from Alexandria who had come to Ephesus where he spoke fearlessly about Christ's "new way" in the Jewish synagogue, although he knew "only of John's baptism." Two women, Priscilla and Aquila, heard him and were so impressed that they took him home and "explained to him God's new way in greater detail." (That fact may tell us something about the important position of women in the early Church.) It is most interesting that Apollos "went about establishing from the Scriptures that Jesus is the Messiah."

In the gospel Jesus and his apostles are still at the Last Supper. He gives them some valuable instruction on prayer: Whatever we ask the Father *in Jesus' name* will be granted—an insight that the Church in her official prayers has never forgotten. The reader alone knows how well he or she has observed Christ's directive:

> Ask and you shall receive,
> that your joy may be full.

After telling us that we are loved by the Father because we have loved him, our Lord utters this briefest of autobiographies:

> I came from God . . .
> I came into the world.
> Now I am leaving the world
> to go to the Father.

Looking back over the past half year since Christmas, it should not be too difficult for us to fill in the details of Christ's life that he left out here (try doing it; in itself that would be an excellent kind of prayer), and we praise and bless him for having allowed us to share his life now made present for us in our daily and Sunday liturgies.

The Communion Antiphon takes us into the next chapter of John's gospel, and we hear Jesus pray to the Father for his apostles:

> Father, I want the men you have given me to be with me where I am, so that they may see the glory you have given me, alleluia.

In our liturgical participation we are with Jesus, and he is with us, and that is wonderful. But we need more, and we pray for it in the prayer that ends the Mass:

> Lord,
> may this eucharist,
> which we have celebrated in memory of your Son,
> help us to grow in love.
> We ask this in the name of Jesus the Lord.

Knowledge—even of Jesus and his life—without love for him and our neighbor is fruitless, so there could hardly be a more necessary prayer.

60   SEVENTH SUNDAY OF EASTER   Cycle A

READING I   Acts 1:12-14   **READING II**   1 Pet 4:13-16
GOSPEL   John 17:1-11

Reading I: After Jesus' ascension the apostles return to Jerusalem to the upper room, where together with Mary and the other women they devoted themselves to prayer.

Reading II: Peter tells us that as Christians we share in the sufferings of Christ, and we ought not be ashamed.

Gospel: This contains the conclusion of Jesus' "high priestly" prayer to the Father at the Last Supper, a prayer for the apostles and all who follow them.

> Lord, hear my voice when I call to you. My heart has prompted me to seek your face; I seek it, Lord; do not hide from me, alleluia (Entrance Antiphon).

I have often compared today's Mass to the Advent season, with its pervading theme of hope and longing desire. The apostles really believe in Jesus' promises, but now they have to exchange the reality of his physical presence for his presence in promise. So for nine days all they can do is wait, pray, and hope—and not only they but the small community of Christ's followers, with Mary the heart of the group.

> Hear, O Lord, the sound of my call;
> have pity on me, and answer me.
> Of you my heart speaks; you my glance seeks (Responsorial Psalm).

This might have been their prayer then; it is ours now. May it fill all our hearts to overflowing. With some reflection and a bit of remembering, we can cram all the longing of four weeks of Advent into this Mass today, and at the same time we can prepare ourselves for the aftermath of the coming of the Holy Spirit promised us by Christ.

All of his life Jesus revealed the incredible good news that our God is a loving, gracious, forgiving God who loves us infinitely and wants us to be with him forever. Jesus prays to this God, his and our Father, and he wants us to share his prayer. He wants us also to spread around what we hear:

> I entrusted to them
> the message you entrusted to me . . . .
> I am in the world no more,
> but these are in the world.

Today we hope in God and in the fulfillment of Jesus' promises. It is good to be reminded that our hope in God is insignificant compared to his hope in us and his trust that we will be open to the coming invasion of hearts by the Holy Spirit. We will respond to that invasion and we will be fearless in sharing the same good news that Jesus shared with us.

> Father,
> help us to keep in mind that Christ our Savior
> lives with you in glory
> and promised to remain with us until the end of time (Opening Prayer).

Remaining with us till the end of time, Jesus makes all of life holy. Our life cannot be ordinary. Christ in us cannot be static. He expects us to grow and to develop our humanity to its fullest extent, by developing our talents and by learning to value the good and the beautiful everywhere around us, especially in other people. Each of us is different, but each of us possesses Christ in his or her own way. We do not, we cannot, live in a vacuum by ourselves. We need one another. It is as if Jesus said to us: "If you want to come to me, learn to give of yourself to others, as I have given myself to you."

A French journalist for the magazine *La Vie Catholique* once asked a number of people when they felt themselves to be closest to God. One person answered: "I feel closer to God when I attend to the needs of the sick and the very poor. For God is there." I am sure we could include the aged in that list of "God-givers."

If we can compare this Sunday and week with all of Advent, we might also think of Pentecost—the fulfillment of today's longing—along with Christmas and Epiphany. But Pentecost is even more; it is the fulfillment of all the meaning contained in the birth of Jesus and all of his life's work. It is the fulfillment of all our hearts' desires, of all the desires of our suffering brothers and sisters everywhere.

So we believe Jesus when he promises:

> I will not leave you orphans.
> I will come back to you, and your hearts will rejoice (Gospel Verse).

> Hear, O Lord, the sound of my call; . . . .
> of you my heart speaks; . . . .
> Hide not your face from me (Responsorial Psalm).

61 SEVENTH SUNDAY OF EASTER Cycle B

READING I Acts 1:15-17, 20-26   **READING II** 1 John 4:11-16
GOSPEL John 17:11-19

Reading I: Returning to the upper room after the ascension, Peter presides over the choice of Matthias as the replacement for Judas.

Reading II: Love of God manifested in love for neighbor is the necessary force that binds a community together.

Gospel: About to go off to his death, Jesus prays for his apostles, begging the Father to protect them from the evil one and to consecrate them by means of truth.

Today's readings inevitably take us back to the Last Supper and to the activities of the one hundred and twenty brothers and sisters in the upper room immediately after the ascension of the Lord. We may even find it profitable to use our imaginations to enable us to enter into the minds of that group, especially those of its core members, the apostles. But first to the practical work to be done, the choice of a successor to the ill-fated defector and traitor, Judas.

The method of election is interesting. Peter takes over, introduces the problem, and lays down the condition for the selection; the new apostle must be "a witness with us to his resurrection." Then they pray that God will make his choice known to them. They draw lots between Joseph (called Barsabbas) and Matthias. The latter is chosen and "added to the eleven apostles."

We can imagine that the entire group did a lot of praying during those nine novena days between Ascension and Pentecost, a lot of wondering and speculating about what Jesus' promise of the "Spirit of Truth" will be like, and perhaps most of all, a lot of indulging in memories—memories of how he first called them; their wanderings through Galilee; his walking on the water; his multiplying the loaves and fishes; the very slow progress they made in coming to know him; how they gradually grew in love for him; the mistakes they made; the encounters with the legalistic Pharisees and Scribes; that awful final week; the Last Supper; the crucifixion; the resurrection and his first appearance to them in this same room; and finally the ascension.

Do we wonder if they were confused, bewildered, anxious, but also hopeful, full of wonderment and eager expectation? Probably they had many questions for Mary, the one who knew him best and for the longest time.

There is a sense of Christ's absence in today's liturgy. It may be good for us to experience a feeling of absence. It is like our psychological and emotional feeling during Advent, with all its longing desire for the Savior, for filling up the bottomless abysses of our hungry hearts.

Today and all of next week is like Advent compressed into a few days.

> Lord, hear my voice when I call to you. My heart has prompted me to seek your face; I seek it, Lord; do not hide from me (Entrance Antiphon).

Today's Opening Prayer puts our longing into words and at the same time also provides some comfort for us:

> Father,
> help us keep in mind that Christ our Savior
> lives with you in glory
> and promised to remain with us until the end of time.

That is all; just help us *keep in mind* (not just *remember*, but keep on remembering, never let the memory fade; the words of Deuteronomy are even more expressive: "fix in your hearts" [4:38]) that Jesus lives in glory and at the same time promised to remain with us until the end of time. Only he can "bilocate" like that.

As long as we are praying, we can become practical and beg: Help us to keep in mind and fix in our hearts that Christ's words and commission to the apostles are intended for us:

> As you [Father] have sent me into the world,
> so I have sent them into the world (Gospel).

The Lord has called each of us to live in our world not as tourists but for one chief reason, to be *witnesses to the resurrection*, that is to proclaim the reality of Jesus' resurrection in our lives by the newness of our lives. Then, too, in a more active way we witness to the reality of the resurrection by sharing the good news with others and by making the presence of the living God visible in the world (Monika Hellwig).

Reading II gives us the way—the only way—to be effective witnesses to the resurrection:

> Beloved,
> if God has loved us so [that he gave his only Son],
> we must have the same love for one another.
> No one has ever seen God.
> Yet if we love one another
> *God dwells in us,*
> *and his love is brought to perfection in us* (italics mine).

To carry out this God-given call and to fulfill its condition for success—genuine love for one another—is impossible by our own powers alone. Now perhaps we understand our need for the Holy Spirit. Now we can make our own the prayer of that first Christian community during their interlude between Ascension and Pentecost:

> My heart has prompted me to seek your face; I seek it, Lord; do not hide from me (Entrance Antiphon).

And we can add:

> God our Savior,
> hear us,
> and through this holy mystery give us hope
> that the glory you have given Christ
> will be given to the Church, his body,
> for he is Lord for ever and ever (Prayer after Communion).

Amen.

62 SEVENTH SUNDAY OF EASTER   Cycle C

READING I Acts 7:55-60   **READING II** Rev 22:12-14, 16-17, 20
GOSPEL John 17:20-26

Reading I: This gives the account of the martyrdom of the first martyr, Stephen, and his prayer for forgiveness for his executioners.

Reading II: We hear about John's vision of the end of time. Jesus says in the vision: "Remember, I am coming soon!" Amen. Come, Lord Jesus!

Gospel: The end of Christ's high priestly prayer at the Last Supper is given. This is a prayer not only for the apostles but for all who will believe in Jesus: "that all may be one."

After the ascension the apostles return to the upper room and are joined by some one hundred and twenty followers of Christ including Mary, Jesus' mother. Jesus had promised them: "I will not leave you orphans. I will come back to you, and your hearts shall rejoice." He had also promised to send them the "Spirit of truth, who would teach them all things." They may well wonder during the novena of prayer and expectation between Ascension and Pentecost just what and whom to expect. They live in faith and great longing. The words of today's Reading II, written by John some sixty or seventy years later, could well have expressed their feelings: "The Spirit and the Bride say, 'Come!' Let him who hears answer, 'Come!' . . . . The One who gives this testimony says, 'Yes, I am coming soon!' Amen! Come, Lord Jesus!"

"Come, Lord Jesus!" was our Advent prayer, too. So we have the same sentiment in today's Entrance Antiphon:

> Lord, hear my voice when I call to you. My heart has prompted me to seek your face; I seek it, Lord; do not hide from me, alleluia.

The real inner desire and hunger expressed in today's Mass are perhaps more necessary now than they were then. Our longing is for the fulfillment of Christ's promises at the Last Supper in our lives, our world. We and our world need the fulfillment of Christ's promise of the Holy Spirit as counselor, as comforter, as instructor of hearts to complete Christ's work in us and our world and bring that work to its ultimate conclusion. The Spirit alone can heal the wounds of division that torment our world and threaten to destroy it, that divide churches, families, parishes, communities.

At the Last Supper Jesus revealed the deepest desire of his heart in his final prayer:

> I do not pray for [my disciples] alone.
> I pray also for those who will believe
> in me through their word,
> *that all may be one*
> *as you, Father, are in me, and I in you;*
> *I pray that they may be [one] in us* (italics mine).

And then comes the real purpose of his desire for unity among his own: "that the world may believe that you sent me." In other words the best and ultimately the only truly effective argument for the spread of Christianity in the world is unity among those who profess to follow Christ.

It is a truth of Christian history that unity among Christ's followers has never been easy to bring about. Already in the communities founded by Paul there were divisions, so that Paul once cried out in anguish: "Has Christ, then, been divided into parts?" (1 Cor 1:13). And we can well imagine non-Christians asking the same question today. It ought to be the most painful and distressing question that we Christians could possibly hear. Unfortunately all too many seem totally indifferent to it. And quite naturally they always blame everybody else. "I'm right. No question about that."

We might wonder what Stephen, the first martyr, would say about that attitude. As he was being stoned to death, he prayed for his executioners: "Lord, do not hold this sin against them" (Reading I). We may rightly surmise that Stephen's loving forgiveness was responsible for the ultimate conversion of the "young man named Saul" who witnessed the martyrdom. Love, especially forgiving love, generates grace.

We should never tire of hearing and reading what Pope John XXIII said at the opening of the Second Vatican Council. He was speaking to both Protestant observers and to the bishops: "We do not wish to put anyone in history on trial; we do not seek to establish who was right and who was wrong. Responsibility is divided. We only wish to say: Let us come together, let us put an end to our divisions!"

Every Mass we share in brings Christ's prayer for unity home to us. In each of the Eucharistic Prayers of the Mass, the priest prays in the name of all:

> May all of us who share in the body and blood of Christ
> be brought together in unity by the Holy Spirit.
> Lord, remember your Church throughout the world;
> make us grow in love.

This is the prayer of Jesus: that his believers may become one as he is one with the Father (Communion Antiphon).

When the prayer of Christ becomes our prayer, and when we beg the Holy Spirit to remove from our hearts any attitudes that divide us from our fellow Christians, Christ's prayer will be answered. Come, Holy Spirit of love and forgiveness! Come!

297 MONDAY OF THE SEVENTH WEEK OF EASTER

READING I Acts 19:1-8
GOSPEL John 16:29-33

Reading I: Paul runs into a group of disciples at Ephesus who had been baptized by John. He baptizes them in the name of the Lord Jesus, and they receive the Holy Spirit.

Gospel: Here we have the conclusion of Jesus' discourse with the apostles at the Last Supper. He tells them that they will suffer. "But take courage! I have overcome the world."

This entire week is one of intense preoccupation with the Holy Spirit and the "arrival" of the Spirit next Sunday. Preoccupation with the vital presence of the Spirit was very much a part of the life of the first Christians. How could they ever forget that it was the Holy Spirit who actually made them Christians in the fullest sense of the word. But we might wonder if their preoccupation with the Holy Spirit was not actually the Spirit's ongoing preoccupation with them.

The Entrance Antiphon takes us back to the very moment of Jesus' ascent to the Father. We hear him speaking to his apostles:

> You will receive power when the Holy Spirit comes upon you. You will be my witnesses to all the world.

The promise spoken by Jesus then is now intended for us, and as they awaited the fulfillment of that promise, so do we look forward to its fulfillment in our lives next Sunday. "Come, Holy Spirit!"

The Opening Prayer indicates the awareness of our personal need for the Spirit.

> Lord,
> send the power [again that word!] of your Holy Spirit upon us
> that we may remain faithful
> and do your will in our daily lives.

Those two petitions can easily be interchanged. Is not doing God's will in daily life the best way of remaining faithful to the way of life Jesus has laid out for us in the Gospels?

Reading I illustrates the preoccupation with the Holy Spirit that has already been mentioned. Only now it is evident in the manner Paul presents the faith to the Ephesians. His first question was: "Did you receive the Holy Spirit when you became believers?" They reply: "We have not so much as heard that there is a Holy Spirit." Obviously not, since the Spirit was not part of the preaching of John the Baptizer, as Paul explains. So he baptizes them, and it is interesting that his ritual included the laying on of hands, which is now used in the ritual of all the sacraments. Apparently present-day baptism seldom results in the recipients being able to speak in tongues. What is more essential is that new converts enter into the apostolic ministry of spreading the faith by their example and by rejoicing in their new life.

The Responsorial Psalm responds both to the reading and to the recent ascension of the Lord:

> Sing to God, O kingdoms of the earth . . .
> Sing to God, chant praise to his name,
> whose name is the Lord;
> exult before him.

Good advice in any age and at all times!

The gospel records John's memory of the closing portion of Jesus' loving conference to his apostles at the Last Supper. He has been voicing a lot of mysterious ideas, has been giving them advice on how to carry out their commission, revealing his relationship with the Father, and promising to send them the Holy Spirit. Now they *think* they understand him: "At last you are speaking plainly. . . . We are convinced that you know everything. . . . We do indeed believe you came from God."

Jesus knows better. He predicts their desertion, their leaving him alone. What must they have thought when he predicted their own future:

> You will suffer in the world.
> But take courage!
> I have overcome the world.

That prediction is also meant for us, and we can all undoubtedly verify its fulfillment in our own lives. How much do the apostles and we need another of Jesus' promises at that Last Supper: "I will not leave you orphans. I will come back to you, and your hearts will rejoice."

As usual the Prayer after Communion is practical, it fits the needs of daily life:

> Merciful Father,
> may these mysteries [lovely name for the Mass!] give us new purpose and bring us to a new life in you.

Do we need new purpose? Yes, if the goals of living are selfish. Yes, if the values by which we live are cheap and materialistic. Yes, if our life is in no way beneficial to the Church, to society, to humankind. It may well be that every one of us needs to say AMEN to that prayer.

298 TUESDAY OF THE SEVENTH WEEK OF EASTER

READING I Acts 20:17-27
GOSPEL John 17:1-11

Reading I: Paul tells the elders of the Church at Ephesus that his missionary activity is going to give way to a new phase in his life, that of suffering and eventually dying for the Faith.

Gospel: This reading consists of Jesus' high priestly prayer to the Father at the Last Supper, a prayer for the disciples to whom he has entrusted his truth.

It seems that all of Paul's life after his conversion was characterized by journeying. He was on his way from Jerusalem to Damascus when he was miraculously converted, and after being finally accepted by the Church (after a journey to the Arabian desert for a "retreat") his life consisted of journeying from city to city establishing churches for Christ. He even intended to go to Spain to preach the Gospel, but the Holy Spirit had other plans for him.

In today's first reading he is on his way to Jerusalem, "compelled by the Spirit," who was obviously very real to him, not knowing what will happen to him there except that "the Holy Spirit has been warning me from city to city that chains and hardships await me." We can conjecture if Paul enjoyed all that "compelling." It is surely certain that he went along with it.

Today we pray that the Father will send that same Holy Spirit

> to live in our hearts
> and make us temples of his glory (Opening Prayer).

A most extraordinary prayer, when you think of all its implications, but it is not without foundation. Paul himself tells us: "Are you not aware that you are the temple of God, and that the Spirit of God dwells in you? If anyone destroys God's temple, God will destroy him. For the temple of God is holy, and you are that temple" (1 Cor 3:16-17). Priests and teachers like to use that thought in counselling young people about the tragic danger of injuring and even destroying the temple of the human body by drugs, tobacco, alcohol, or the unlawful enjoyment of sex.

We respond to Reading I by recalling another biblical and natural image of the Holy Spirit: "A bountiful rain you showered down, O God, upon your inheritance; you restored the land when it languished." Without the Spirit our hearts are like a drought-stricken land. Nothing can grow on it; its topsoil blows away with the slightest wind. But see what happens when a bountiful rain falls on it! The land is reborn; it becomes a rich mine of nourishment for the needy.

> Blessed day by day be the Lord,
> who bears our burdens; God, who
> is our salvation (Responsorial Psalm).

Come, Holy Spirit, bring to life the dry land of our hearts!

The gospel brings us the beginning of Jesus' high priestly prayer to the Father after he has finished instructing the apostles at the Last Supper:

> Father, the hour has come!
> Give glory to your Son
> that your Son may give glory to you.

That prayer will surely be heard but not before the torturous passion and death that lies just ahead of him. Jesus lets us in on a fascinating theological conception of what heaven will be like when he says:

> Eternal life is this:
> *to know you*, the only true God,
> and him whom you have sent, Jesus Christ (italics mine).

Knowing God may not sound very exciting and desirable to many jaded hearts, until they realize that hunger for knowledge is one of the deepest desires of our hearts. Without it there would be no libraries, newspapers, magazines, TV, or any other news media. But the knowledge Jesus speaks of, which our departed loved ones now enjoy in heaven, is knowledge of God permeated with love. It will simultaneously leave us satisfied *and* full of desire to know ever more and more the God who is its inexhaustible source.

Jesus prays not only for himself but also for these men with whom he entrusted his message. We can imagine Jesus thinking in his heart how human and vulnerable they are—how they and my followers through all ages will need our help and guidance: "these are in the world as I come to you. There will never be a time when they will not need our help; we must be with them always."

So he promises:

> the Holy Spirit whom the Father will send in my name will teach you all things, and remind you of all I have said to you (Communion Antiphon).

Our response is a prayer:

> Lord,
> may this eucharist, which we have celebrated in memory of your Son, help us to grow in love (Prayer after Communion).

Love—for Jesus and for one another—is the greatest of all our needs. May the Holy Spirit grant our prayer!

299 WEDNESDAY OF THE SEVENTH WEEK OF EASTER

READING I Acts 20:28-38
GOSPEL John 17:11-19

Reading I: We share in a magnificent farewell Paul addresses to the elders of the Church of Ephesus: "I commend you now to the Lord, and to that gracious word of his which can enlarge you."

Gospel: Jesus continues his prayer for the apostles: "protect them . . . that they may be one, even as we are one."

Yesterday Jesus opened our worship with the triumphal declaration:

> I am the beginning and the end of all things. I have met death, but I am alive, and I shall live for eternity (Entrance Antiphon).

We know how right he is, so today we cry out:

> All nations, clap your hands. Shout with a voice of joy to God, alleluia (Entrance Antiphon).

Tragically all nations will refuse to accept that invitation. Many will not even know what we are talking about, and many people who call themselves Christian are divided in their understanding of Jesus, of his redeeming work, of his teaching. There is perhaps no greater need in our world than a united Christianity if it is to carry out Christ's task. So we pray:

> God of mercy,
> unite your Church in the Holy Spirit
> that we may serve you with all our hearts
> and work together with unselfish love.

Every word in that prayer is essential. When self predominates in our philosophy of life, personal service in response to Jesus' love is in danger of vanishing, and the missionary work of Christ's Church becomes ineffective.

Paul realized this and his instruction—originally to the elders of the Church of Ephesus and now to us—comes out of his personal experience. He warns against men who will distort the truth and lead astray Jesus' followers with the result of inevitable division in the Christian community. There is no more deadly obstacle to the spread of the Gospel than divisiveness among those who claim to be Christian. So our prayer today is probably the most crucial of the entire week.

Paul's review of his life as a missionary may seem somewhat vain to us, but true humility does not imply or demand a downgrading of self and one's accomplishments. Vanity dominates our lives when we take all the credit for our accomplishments to ourselves, with no acknowledgement of the help of God and the contributions of others to our successes. Paul realizes that his accomplishments in spreading the Gospel have been excellent. He knows the truth about himself, but he recognizes that whatever success he has had has simply been a response to the grace that the Lord has constantly made available to him. He ends his words to his friends by reminding them that "there is more happiness in giving than receiving."

The touching response of the people indicates how much they have come to value Paul's sacrifices in bringing Christ and the Gospel to them. He has taught them well, they weep, they embrace him, but then they escort him to the ship and give him back to God.

Today's gospel continues Jesus' prayer, his communing *with* the Father *for* the apostles. He expresses his concern for their spiritual welfare and his concern about the dangers they will encounter in carrying out his commission to them. His greatest worry is that the spirit of the world—worldliness—will obscure or destroy their primary aim of preaching the Word:

> I do not ask you to take them out
> of the world,
> but to guard them from the evil one.

The help he pleads for is that the Father will "consecrate them by means of truth—'Your word is truth.'"

I take that to mean that it is God's grace-filled Word that will keep them loyal, with eyes fixed on the same goal for which both Jesus and Paul will give their lives. We may not forget that everything Jesus prays for here *is also meant for us.*

> I consecrate myself for their sakes now,
> that they may be consecrated in truth.

We need much help in doing our share in fulfilling Christ's will for us, so we pray:

> May these sacred mysteries by which we worship you
> bring your salvation to perfection within us (Prayer over the Gifts).

Best of all we can take comfort in our Lord's promise:

> When the Holy Spirit comes to you, the Spirit whom I shall send, . . .
> he will bear witness to me, and you also will be my witnesses, alleluia (Communion Antiphon).

Alleluia, Alleluia, Alleluia!

300 THURSDAY OF THE SEVENTH WEEK OF EASTER

READING I Acts 22:30; 23:6-11
GOSPEL John 17:20-26

Reading I: In Jerusalem the Sanhedrin puts Paul on trial, but he professes his belief in the resurrection of the dead and creates a conflict between the Pharisees (who believe) and the Sadducees (who do not).

Gospel: We have the conclusion of Jesus' prayer at the Last Supper: "I pray that they may be [one]."

Today's gospel comes at the end of Jesus' prayer and discourse at the Last Supper. Of special concern to us Christians living now is his prayer:

> I do not pray for them [my disciples] alone.
> I pray also for those who will believe
> in me through their word,
> that all may be one
> as you, Father, are in me, and I in you;
> I pray that they may be [one] in us,
> *that the world may believe that you sent me.*
> I have given them the glory you gave me
> that they may be one, as we are one . . .
> that their unity may be complete   (italics mine).

So this is Christ's legacy to his Church. We may well wonder how effective his prayer has been and is now. We seem to think of divided Christianity as normal. Yet the hundreds of different denominations all claiming to be Christian, the divisions within each denomination, including our own Roman Catholic Church, similar divisions in our own parishes, religious communities, and families cause us to ask ourselves: In the context of Christ's prayer, can this be what he wants? The answer seems to be that—powerful though Christ's prayer was—it is within the scandalous potential of Christians to render that prayer powerless. The result is that the world, in the form of millions of nonbelievers, does not believe that Jesus was sent by the Father and does not even consider him a religious leader to be taken seriously.

This gospel ought to shock everyone who hears it, but it seems we are so accustomed to it that we feel it does not really apply to our situation. Besides did not Christ himself declare: "My mission is to spread, not peace, but division" (Matt 10:34)? The answer to that question is that Jesus does not tell us here that he *wants* turmoil and antagonism among those for whom he died, but that human perversity uses him as an argument for one side or the other. Or they do not really understand his Word.

God knows, and we all know from experience, that making peace is a never-ending struggle. Peace does have to be *made*, it does not just happen. We often wonder if there will ever be unity and peace between churches and between Christians. But would Christ propose an impossible ideal? Unity has to be possible or he was a dreamer. It is the obligation of every Christian to work for unity and peace among Christians, to pray, to sacrifice, to be willing if necessary to lay down one's life for that noble goal—as Jesus himself did. Maybe ultimate success will come only at the end of time, but that may not and must not discourage us. The first step may well be to try to convince every Christian who claims to love Jesus that he is serious in praying this prayer: Father, grant that they may be one in us.

I once wrote: "If Jesus desired unity, if he prayed for unity, so must the Christian. But unity will not come unless we do more than talk about it; we must work for it, remove the obstacles within ourselves, pray, suffer. . . . The great French theologian and ecumenist, Fr. Yves Congar, O.P. once said: 'We must pass through the door of ecumenism on our knees' " *(Understanding Our Neighbor's Faith,* Collegeville, Minn.: Liturgical Press, 1975, 279).

This may all sound like a sermon, but hopefully it is also a recapitulation of the meaning and goal of Jesus' life and a preparation for the coming of the Holy Spirit into our hearts next Sunday. Today's prayer is most appropriate and most essential for bringing us to an awareness of our obligations as peacemakers in the name of Jesus our beloved Lord:

> Father,
> let your Spirit come upon us with power
> to fill us with his gifts.
> May he make our hearts pleasing to you,
> and ready to do your will (Opening Prayer).

301 FRIDAY OF THE SEVENTH WEEK OF EASTER

READING I Acts 25:13-21
GOSPEL John 21:15-19

Reading I: Paul is now in Caesaria; he, as a Roman citizen, has appealed his case to the emperor, and he awaits the royal decision.

Gospel: We are with Jesus and the apostles on the shores of the Sea of Galilee after the resurrection. Jesus asks Peter: "do you love me?"

Christ loved us and has washed away our sins with his blood, and has made us a kingdom of priests to serve his God and Father, alleluia (Entrance Antiphon).

It would be hard to find a shorter or more exact summary of Jesus' life and work than that. Motivated entirely by love, Jesus shed his blood for us, washed away our sins, and made us a kingdom of priests to serve his God and Father. Do we ever think of ourselves and our Church as "a kingdom of priests?" This kingdom includes every Christian who is baptized; our service of the Father results from our living lives of mutual love and by caring for the unfortunates of our world.

Yesterday in the gospel we were at the Last Supper listening to Christ's prayer for oneness among his followers. Today, several weeks later, we are present at one of the most touching scenes of the Gospel. Jesus and the apostles are back at one of their most familiar places, the shore of the Sea of Galilee, where he had first called at least some of them to their new life with him.

No doubt they have been indulging in memories, both pleasant and painful, of the day he first called them from their old profession as fishermen, of his having walked on the waters of this same lake, of their three years of following him as they walked the paths of Galilee, drinking in his words, watching him in his healing ministry. There are also the more recent memories of their having forsaken him in his trial and death, and for Peter especially his having denied him three times after swearing he would never forsake him.

They have just had another meal with him, this one prepared by Jesus himself. They have been watching him, and suddenly he looks up and at the man he had called the rock foundation of his Church, the man he had chosen to be first among equals. He asks: "Simon, son of John, do you love me?" Three times he asks and three times Peter answers: "Yes, Lord, you know that I love you." The evangelist tells us that Peter is hurt because Jesus puts the question three times. His being "hurt" is surely putting it mildly, with the haunting memory of his three-fold denial so fresh in his heart. He finally cries out: "Lord, you know everything. You know well that I love you." Jesus then gives him the third commission to feed and tend his lambs and sheep and then predicts the way in which Peter will seal his love, the kind of death he will die.

We know, of course, that as Roman Catholics we believe that this incident is the crowning moment of Jesus' choice of Peter as the head of his Church, that Peter eventually went to Rome, where he established his bishop's see, and that the bishops of Rome have been considered the heads of the Church since his day.

It may or may not be strange that the whole process of Christ's choice of Peter began with questions: "Who do people say that the Son of Man is? Who do you say that I am?" (Matt 16:13-15). And now: "Simon, son of John, do you love me?" It seems that Jesus wants to know, he wants a personal commitment. And he still wants it. Only now he wants it from each of us—Who do *you* say that I am? Do *you* love me?—as a necessary condition for being among his followers.

He wants each of us to answer out of the fullness of our hearts and perhaps against a background of past betrayals of him by our sins.

We are close to the end of the Easter season and are looking forward to receiving the fulfillment of Jesus' promise to send us the Holy Spirit next Sunday. For over half a year we have been following Jesus. Hopefully it has been a time of growing intimacy with Jesus, above all a time of coming to know how much he has loved us. How much, too, we want to love him. Today's prayer is exactly what we need:

> Father,
> in . . . sending us your Spirit,
> you open the way to eternal life.
> May our sharing in this gift increase our love
> and make our faith grow stronger (Opening Prayer).

"Bless the Lord, O my soul" (Responsorial Psalm).

302 SATURDAY OF THE SEVENTH WEEK OF EASTER

READING I Acts 28:16-20, 30-31
GOSPEL John 21:20-25

Reading I: Paul is now in prison in Rome, but people come to him and he continues to preach the Gospel.

Gospel: Peter follows after Jesus but then wonders about John; Jesus tells him: "Your business is to follow me."

We have been celebrating the love of Christ for the last seven weeks (see Opening Prayer), and now we are at the eve of what might well be the most dramatic event in the history of the world, the coming of the Holy Spirit upon the Church. Today's Entrance Antiphon returns us to the upper room where

> The disciples were constantly at prayer together, with Mary the mother of Jesus, the other women, and the brothers of Jesus.

They have had the promise of Jesus that he would send them the Spirit of truth who will lead them to the whole truth (see the Gospel Verse), but they have no idea what that coming will be like.

What is of special interest is the presence of Mary, of the other women followers of Jesus, and his relatives. It is a kind of miniature of the Church that is to come out of tomorrow's fulfillment of Jesus' promise. Up to now they have all been individuals; after tomorrow they will be a single organism, with the Holy Spirit as the life principle.

All this took place "back then." Today's prayer brings us to "now."

> Let the love we have celebrated in this Easter season
> be put into practice in our daily lives (Opening Prayer).

That is it: short and to the point. We can dream about God's love for us in Christ, write poetry about it, even become sentimental, but unless and until the love of Christ that impelled him to die for us becomes incarnate in our daily lives, it remains only a dream that is quite useless. The best way to further its growth in us is to celebrate it as often as possible in the Eucharist, together with a ceaseless prayer to the Holy Spirit whom Jesus promised and who is always available for the asking. Without the Holy Spirit all human effort to live up to our obligations as Christians is quite futile. So, "Come, Holy Spirit, fill all our hearts!"

Today's Reading I and the gospel seem to have little relationship to tomorrow's great happening. Reading I again gives us Paul, now in Rome, where he is allowed to live on his own in a rented lodging, "although a soldier was assigned to keep guard over him." He meets with Jewish leaders in the city and tries to justify himself against the false charges of the leaders in Jerusalem. Today's reading does not record the success he had, but the omitted verses tell us how they invite him to tell them about the Gospel he preaches, and some are even converted. Paul remains in Rome for two years doing what he does best, preaching the reign of God inaugurated by his beloved Master Jesus. This is the end of Acts; we are not told how long after the two years are up that Paul's long, fruitful apostolate will be crowned by his martyrdom.

Peter, as the saying goes, is "something else." We recall yesterday's dramatic exclamation of his love for Jesus, his being confirmed in his primacy over the Church, and Jesus' summons: "Follow me." Today's gospel tells us that the following has begun, but suddenly Peter turns around and sees "the disciple whom Jesus loved" also following. So Peter asks Jesus: "But Lord, what about him?" What is it with Peter? Is he envious of John's obvious favored place in Jesus' heart? Does he see him as a possible rival? We just do not know, and neither Jesus nor the commentators are of much help. Jesus says simply: "Suppose I want him to stay until I come . . . how does that concern you?"

Jesus seems to be telling Peter that he (Jesus) is still in charge and that Peter's main task is to follow him. We know, too, that the "following" will end in Rome where Peter will be crucified head down in fulfillment of Jesus' prophecy in yesterday's gospel.

Jesus knew what he was doing when he chose Peter to be the first head of his Church—Peter, the most "human" of the apostles, vulnerable, capable of cowardice, but also capable of great love and ultimate martyrdom. The Church is to be a Church of sinners for sinners—that is, men and women who have to learn, sometimes the hard way that their ultimate salvation depends only on Christ and the Holy Spirit whom he will send to us tomorrow.

> Father of mercy,
> hear our prayers
> that we may leave our former selves behind
> and serve you with holy and renewed hearts (Prayer after Communion).

PENTECOST SUNDAY

READING I Acts 2:1-11
GOSPEL John 20:19-23
READING II 1 Cor 12:3-7, 12-13

Reading I: We hear the account of the first Christian Pentecost: tongues of fire on the heads of the brethren, noise like a strong wind, and the crowd from various parts of the mideast hear Peter speaking, each hearing "in his own tongue about the marvels God has accomplished."

Reading II: Paul tells of the different ministries in Christ's body in which there are many members but one life principle, the Holy Spirit.

Gospel: Here we have John's account of the first Easter: Jesus appears to the apostles, breathes on them, and confers the Holy Spirit.

Scripture does not provide us with a personality sketch of the Holy Spirit as the Gospels do of Jesus. The inspired writers simply tell us who and what the Spirit is by what the Spirit *does*. We can recall the field of dry bones that becomes a living people when breathed upon by the prophet Ezechiel. And we are familiar with the passage from the prophet Joel which Peter quotes in his sermon on that first Pentecost:

> I will pour out a portion of
> my spirit on all mankind:
> Your sons and daughters shall prophesy,
> your young men shall see visions
> and your old men shall dream dreams (Acts 2:17; see Joel 3:1).

Luke in his Gospel often refers to the influence of the Holy Spirit in the life of Jesus, beginning with the promise of the Angel Gabriel to the Virgin Mary: "The Holy Spirit will come upon you and the power of the Most High will overshadow you" (Luke 1:35). Luke also relates how at the beginning of his public life Jesus is led by the Spirit into the desert for his forty day fast. At his first visit to his home town Nazareth, Jesus claims to be fulfilling the promise of the Spirit foretold by Isaiah:

> The Spirit of the Lord is upon me;
> therefore he has anointed me.
> He has sent me to bring glad tidings
> to the poor (Luke 4:18; see Isaiah 61:1).

But it is John who tells of Jesus' promises of the Holy Spirit at the Last Supper. Jesus calls the Spirit the Counsellor, the Spirit of Truth, the Advocate, the Paraclete, who will teach the apostles all things and bring to their remembrance all that he himself has said to them.

So the Spirit is creative, gives life, brings the fullness of truth, and remembers all that Jesus has said. And we know from the story of the first Pentecost which we have in Reading I how the Spirit changed the fear-filled, mystified, ununderstanding apostles into a living community, the Body of Christ (Reading II), completely fired up with the love of Christ and with the irrepressible determination to tell all the world about the Lord Jesus.

Today we *celebrate* divine love. We celebrate all the dynamic activity of the Holy Spirit, from the moment of the Spirit's coming upon the Virgin Mary, leading Jesus during his public life, and finally animating the infant Church and directing all the apostolic labors of the apostles into Gentile lands. It is good to remind ourselves that liturgical celebration, unlike any other recalling of past events, actually *makes present* the original event. So today our churches and chapels are the upper room, and the Holy Spirit is about to come upon us with all the power of that first Pentecost.

What should Pentecost be for us today? First of all, it should bring us *Shalom*, that same *peace* that Jesus gave to those in the upper room; then an increase in gratitude to God for having chosen us to be members of his Body; a greater awareness of our being members of a missionary Church whose work is far from finished; and a greater concern for building up the Body of Christ—the entire, worldwide Church and this particular church or community of which we are members—by promoting reconciliation, forgiveness, and a sense of unity.

Shalom, Christ's gift to the apostles and to us today involves greater completeness in our lives and a full development of all our human potential and talents. It means *joy*, which ought to be the distinguishing mark of the redeemed Christian. Christ offers this gift of "Shalom-Peace" to us today. It will become what he intends it to be only if we accept it and respond to it with joyous hearts.

> Father of light, from whom every good gift comes,
> send your Spirit into our lives
> with the power of a mighty wind,
> and by the flame of your wisdom
> open the horizons of our minds.
> Loosen our tongues to sing your praise
> in words beyond the power of speech,
> for without your Spirit
> man could never raise his voice in words of peace
> or announce the truth that Jesus is Lord (Alternative Opening Prayer).

The original Pentecost brought about a dramatic change in the apostles. We recall their failure to understand Jesus, their fear, and their unhealthy personal ambitions *before* Pentecost. The essential meaning of Pentecost is still change for us, change in people's hearts, in their lack of understanding, their human relationships, their failure to forgive, their pessimism, and their lack of hope. We need the recreated minds and hearts that this feast provides for all who are willing to open their hearts to the Spirit.

Pentecost is still going on in our world, going on wherever the Gospel is being preached, wherever a sacrament is administered, wherever people live and pray together. We are involved in the completion of Christ's work, all of us. The Holy Spirit will never allow us to forget that truth, for we do not possess the Holy Spirit; the Holy Spirit possesses us.

***

The Preface of today's Mass tells us that the Father's sending the Holy Spirit "brought the paschal mystery to its close." From now on it is our privilege, our joy, and our obligation as persons possessed by the Spirit to live out the mystery in our lives.